Project Editor Amanda Wyatt
US Editor Kayla Dugger
Lead Designer Joe Lawrence
Development Editor Ben Morgan
Development Designer Jacqui Swan
Illustrator Clarisse Hassan
Editors Edward Aves, Steven Carton, Alexandra di Falco
Designer Sammi Richiardi
Writers Ben Ffrancon Davies, Junaid Mubeen
Mathematical Consultant Junaid Mubeen
Historical Consultant Philip Parker
Managing Editor Lisa Gillespie
Managing Art Editor Owen Peyton Jones
Producer, Pre-production Robert Dunn
Senior Producer Meskerem Berhane
Jacket Designer Akiko Kato
Jacket Editor Emma Dawson

First American Edition, 2020
Published in the United States by DK Publishing,
a division of Penguin Random House LLC
1745 Broadway, 20th Floor, New York, NY 10019

24 25 26 13 12 11 10 9
055–310504–Jan/2020

Published in Great Britain by Dorling Kindersley Limited

A catalog record for this book
is available from the Library of Congress.
ISBN 978-1-4654-8173-3

Printed and bound in China

www.dk.com

MIX
Paper | Supporting responsible forestry
FSC™ C018179

This book was made with Forest Stewardship Council™ certified paper – one small step in DK's commitment to a sustainable future.
Learn more at
www.dk.com/uk/information/sustainability

WHAT'S THE POINT OF MATH?

CONTENTS

Some dates have BCE and CE after them. These are short for "Before the Common Era" and "Common Era." The Common Era dates from when people think Jesus was born. Where the exact date of an event is not known, "c." is used. This is short for the Latin word *circa*, meaning "around," and indicates that the date is approximate.

WHAT'S THE POINT OF MATH?

Math has an exciting story stretching back many thousands of years. Studying math helps us understand how ideas have evolved throughout human history. From ancient times to today, the human race's incredible progress and advancement owe a lot to our skill and expertise with math.

TELLING TIME

From early humans counting passing days by tracking the moon to today's super-accurate atomic clocks that keep time to tiny fractions of a second, math is with us every second of every hour.

NAVIGATING EARTH

Maths has always helped humans navigate the world, from plotting points on maps to the high-tech triangulation techniques that modern-day GPS systems use.

GROWING CROPS

From early humans trying to predict when fruit would be ripe to modern mathematical analysis that makes sure farmers get the most from their land, math helps feed us all year round.

CREATING ART

How do you create a perfectly proportioned painting or a superbly symmetrical building? Math has the answers—whether it be the ancient Greeks' Golden Ratio or the subtle calculations needed to give a picture perspective.

MAKING MUSIC

Math and music may seem worlds apart, but without math, how could we count a beat or develop a rhythm? Math helps us understand what sounds good, and what doesn't, when different notes fit together to create harmony.

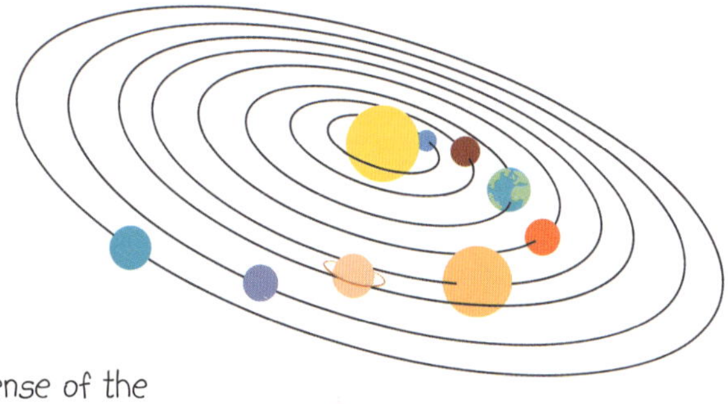

UNDERSTANDING THE UNIVERSE

Math has helped humans make sense of the universe since we first looked up at the night sky. Our early ancestors used tallies to track the phases of the moon. Renaissance scientists studied the planets' orbits. Math is the key to unlocking the secrets of our universe.

DESIGNING AND BUILDING

How do you build something that won't fall down? How do you make it both practical and attractive? Math is the foundation of each decision architects, builders, and engineers make.

EXPLORING SCIENCE

Putting humans, robots, and satellites into space can't be done with guesswork. Astrophysicists need math to precisely calculate orbits and trajectories to safely navigate to the moon and beyond.

SAVING LIVES

Math is literally a lifesaver—whether it's testing a new drug, performing complex operations, or studying a dangerous disease, doctors, nurses, and scientists couldn't save people's lives without a huge amount of mathematical analysis.

MAKING MONEY

From counting what people owned thousands of years ago to the sophisticated mathematical models that explain, manage, and predict international business and trade, our world today could not exist without the mathematics of economics.

COMPUTING

When Ada Lovelace wrote the world's first computer program, she couldn't have imagined the way her math would change the world. Today, our TVs, smartphones, and computers make millions of calculations to allow gigabytes of data to race through high-speed internet connections.

WHAT'S THE POINT OF

NUMBERS AND COUNTING?

Without numbers to count, we wouldn't get very far! From the earliest days of adding up and the simple tally systems our ancestors used, to the algebraic equations used today to explain how the universe works, numbers and counting are as fundamentally important today as they were back when the study of math first began.

HOW TO TRACK TIME

The history of counting goes all the way back to the early humans in Africa, as far back as at least 35,000 years ago. Historians think that our ancestors used straight lines to record the different phases of the Moon and count the number of days passing. This was crucial for their survival as hunter-gatherers—they could now track the movements of herds of animals over time and could even start to predict when certain fruits and berries would become ripe and ready to eat.

3 Early humans did this by keeping a tally—a simple system of lines to record numbers and quantities. By adding new lines, or tally marks, each time they saw the Moon's shape shrink and grow, they had created the world's first type of calendar.

TALLYING

Tally marks are a simple way of counting. The earliest form of this system used straight lines to represent amounts of objects. But this became very difficult to read, especially with high numbers—imagine having to count 100 straight lines to know the number was 100! To make things easier, people began to group the tally marks in fives.

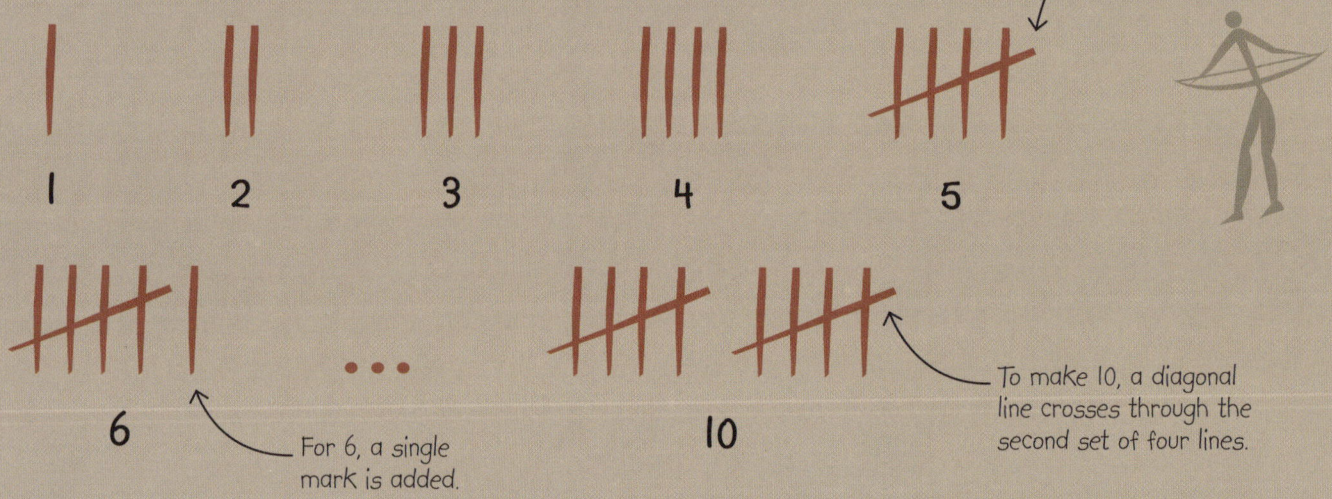

DOT AND LINE TALLYING

Over time, a second system known as dot and line tallying developed. The numbers 1–4 are counted with dots, then lines are added. Eventually, the dots and lines are organized into groups of 10, which is symbolized by a box with dots on each corner and a cross through it.

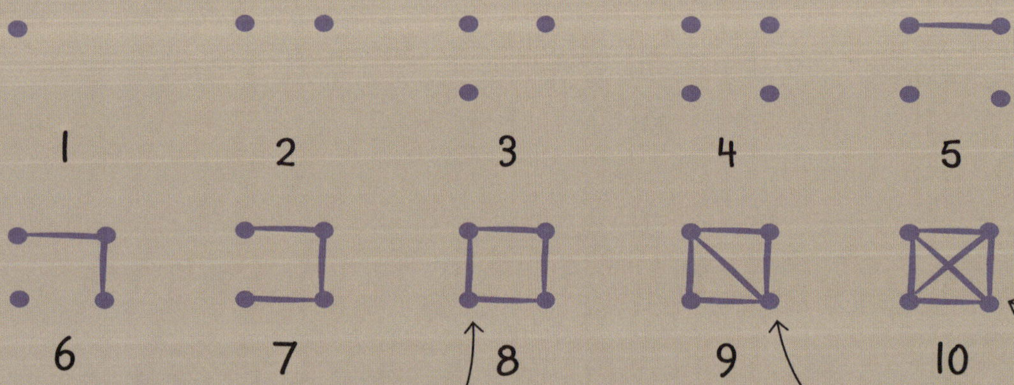

STROKE TALLYING

In China, a different system evolved that uses a Chinese character to count in groups of five. Five is recognizable, as it has a long line across both the top and the bottom.

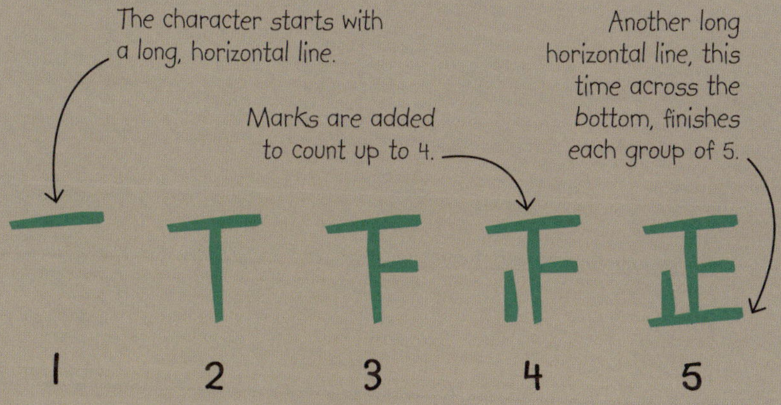

PUZZLE

Can you work out these tallied numbers? Start by counting how many groups of 5 or 10 there are.

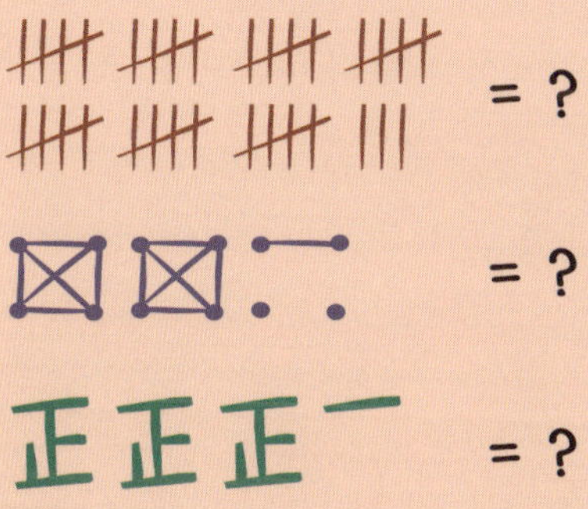

TRY IT OUT

HOW TO TALLY

Tallying is a great way to record the populations of particular animals in an area, such as a yard or park. It works well because you add a new mark for every animal you see instead of rewriting a different number each time.

Try it yourself. Use tally marks to record how many butterflies, birds, and bees you spot in your local area in an hour.

Butterflies	||||
Birds	𝍸 𝍸 |
Bees	𝍸 ||

REAL WORLD

The Ishango bone

This baboon's leg bone was found in 1960 in what is now the Democratic Republic of the Congo. It is more than 20,000 years old and is covered in tally marks. It is one of the earliest surviving physical examples of mathematics being used, but nobody is completely sure what our early human ancestors were recording with the marks.

HOW TO COUNT WITH YOUR NOSE

The first calculator was the human body. Before humans wrote numbers down, they almost certainly counted using their fingers. In fact, the word "digit," which comes from the Latin *digitus*, can still mean both "finger" and "number." Because we have 10 fingers, the counting system most of us use is based on groups of 10, though some civilizations have developed alternative counting systems using different parts of the body—even their noses!

COUNTING IN 10s

Counting with our fingers probably gave rise to the decimal counting system we use today. "Decimal" comes from the Latin word for 10 (*decem*). The decimal system is also known as base-10, which means that we think and count in groups of 10.

COUNTING IN 20s

The Maya and Aztec civilizations of North and Central America used a base-20 counting system. This was probably based on counting with their 10 fingers and 10 toes.

COUNTING IN 60s

The ancient Babylonians used a base-60 system. They probably used the thumb to touch the segments of each finger on one hand, giving them 12, then on the other hand counted up five groups of 12, making 60. Today, we have 60 seconds in a minute and 60 minutes in an hour thanks to the ancient Babylonians.

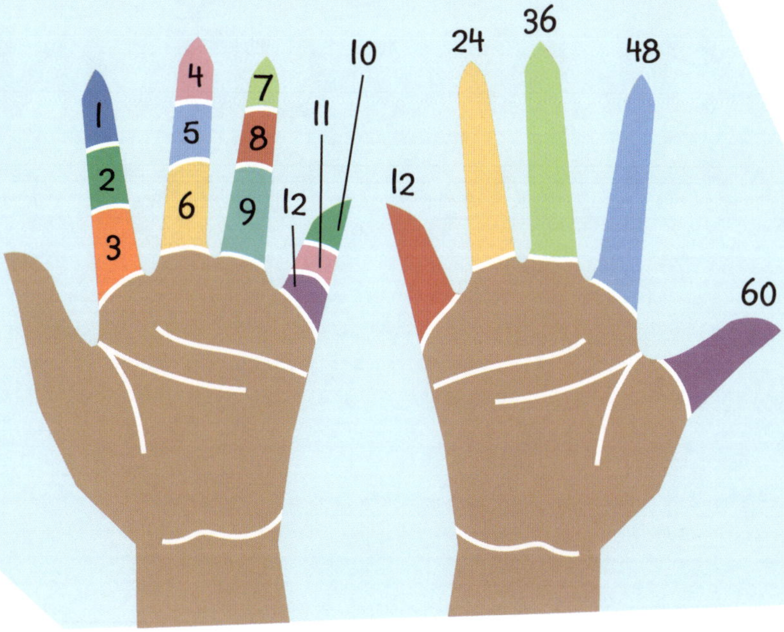

COUNTING IN 27s

Some tribes in Papua New Guinea traditionally use a base-27 system based on body parts. Tribespeople start counting on the fingers on one hand (1–5), go along that arm (6–11), and around the face to the nose (12–14), before running down the other side of the face and body (15–27).

COUNTING WITH ALIENS

If an alien had eight fingers (or tentacles), it would probably count using a base-8 system. It would still be able to do math with this system—its counting would just look different from our decimal system.

HOW TO COUNT YOUR COWS

More than 6,000 years ago, on the fertile plains of Mesopotamia in modern-day Iraq, the Sumerian civilization flourished. More and more people owned land. They grew wheat and kept animals such as sheep and cattle. Sumerian merchants and tax collectors wanted to record what they had traded or how much tax needed to be paid, so they developed a more sophisticated way to count than the tallying methods of our cave-dwelling ancestors or counting using parts of the body.

1 Sumerian merchants and tax collectors wanted to record what they had traded or how much tax had been paid, so they created a system to count and keep track of people's possessions.

2 Small tokens were made out of clay to represent an animal or other common possession. Each person's possessions were counted, and then the appropriate number of tokens was placed inside a hollow, wet clay ball for inspection later. Once the clay ball had dried hard, the tokens inside couldn't be tampered with.

If a merchant or tax collector wanted to find out which tokens were inside a particular ball, the ball had to be broken into pieces.

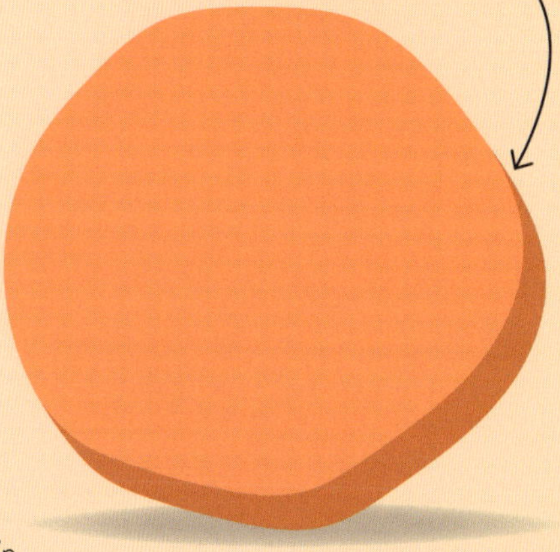

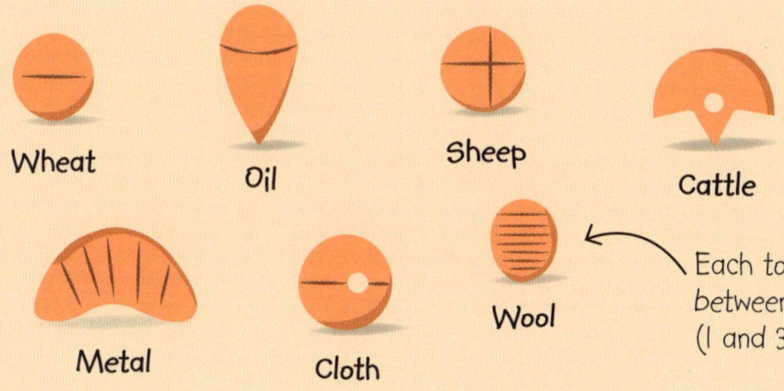

Each token was between ⅓ and 1 in (1 and 3 cm) wide.

3 Eventually, the Sumerians began to use the tokens to press marks onto the outside of a clay ball while it was wet. That way, they didn't have to break it to check which tokens were inside.

4 Later, the people of Mesopotamia took this system a step further—they used symbols to represent numbers, which meant they could record larger quantities of common items and animals.

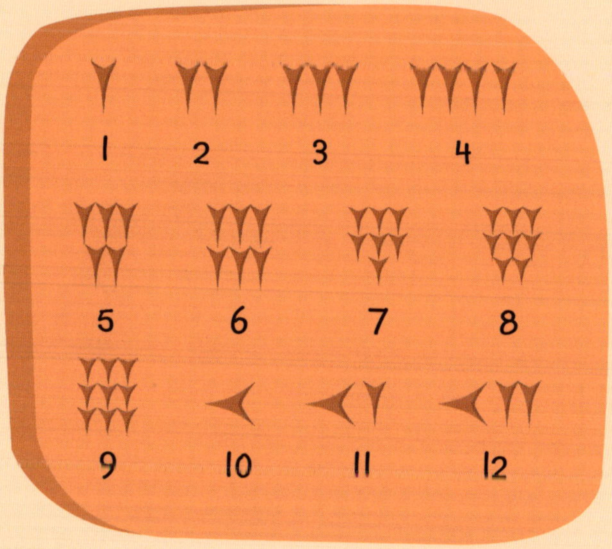

They used a pointed tool called a stylus to write numbers onto clay tablets.

The vertical marks stood for 1 and the horizontal marks were 10, so 12 was made up of one horizontal mark followed by two vertical marks.

ANCIENT NUMBERS

The Sumerians weren't the only ancient civilization to come up with a number system. Lots of societies were finding ways to express numbers. The ancient Egyptians created a number system of their own using their hieroglyphic alphabet, and later the Romans developed a system using letters.

EGYPTIAN HIEROGLYPHICS

The ancient Egyptians used small pictures called hieroglyphics to express words. Around 3000 BCE, they used hieroglyphics to create a number system, with separate numbers for 1, 10, 100, and so on.

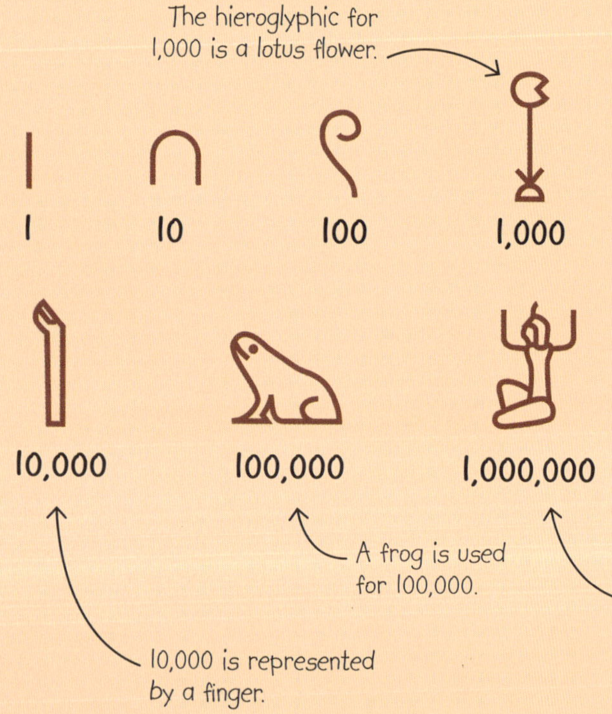

ROMAN NUMERALS

The Romans developed their own numerals using letters. When a smaller numeral appeared after a larger one, it meant that the smaller numeral should be added to the larger one – for example XIII means 10 + 3. If a smaller numeral appeared before a larger one, the smaller numeral should be subtracted – for example, IX is the same as 10 – 1 = 9.

I	II	III	IV	V
1	2	3	4	5
VI	VII	VIII	IX	X
6	7	8	9	10
XX	L	C	D	M
20	50	100	500	1,000

REAL WORLD

Ancient numerals today

Roman numerals are still used today. As well as kings and queens who use them in their titles, like Queen Elizabeth II in the UK, they appear on some clock faces. Sometimes the number 4 is written as IIII on clocks, instead of IV.

NUMBERS TODAY

Brahmi numerals first developed from tally marks in India during the 3rd century BCE. By the 9th century, they had evolved into what became known as Indian numerals. Arabic scholars adopted this system into Western Arabic numerals, which eventually spread to Europe. Over time, a European form of Hindu-Arabic numerals emerged—the most widely used numerical system in the world today.

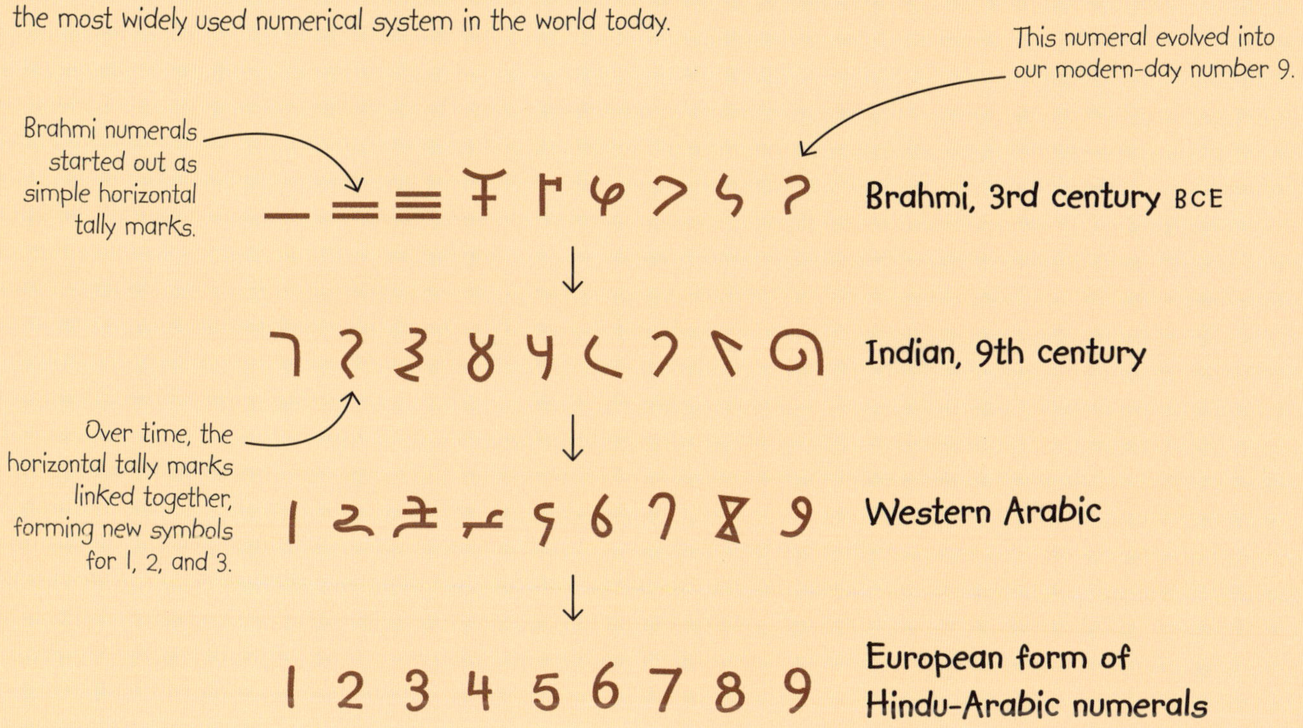

TRY IT OUT

HOW TO WRITE YOUR BIRTHDAY

Famous British Egyptologist Howard Carter was born on May 9, 1874. How would he write his birthday in Egyptian hieroglyphics or Roman numerals?

Egyptian hieroglyphics 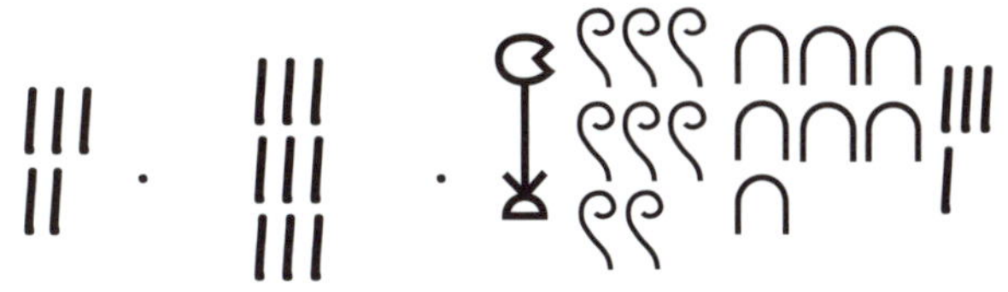

Roman numerals V · IX · MDCCCLXXIV

Now try writing your own birthday in Egyptian hieroglyphics or Roman numerals.

HOW TO MAKE NOTHING A NUMBER

The journey from the abstract idea of "nothing" to the actual number "zero" was a long one, helped along by contributions from civilizations all over the world. Today, the number zero is essential to our modern-day "place value" system, where the position of a numeral in a number tells you its value. For example, in the number 110, 0 stands for how many ones there are, while in the number 101, it stands for how many tens there are. But zero is also a number in its own right—we can add, subtract, and multiply with it.

EMPTY SPACE

The Babylonians were the first people to use a place value system to write out numbers, but they never thought of zero as a number, so they had no numeral for it. Instead, they just left an empty space. But this was confusing, as this meant they wrote numbers like 101 and 1001 in exactly the same way.

11 = 11

1 1 = 101 or 1001?

If 0 didn't exist, it would be hard to know how big a number really is!

2000 BCE

350 BCE

NOTHING AT ALL

The idea of zero never occurred to the Romans since their counting system didn't need one. They used specific letters to represent certain numbers rather than a place value system. This meant that they could write out numbers like 1201 without needing zero: MCCI = 1000 + 100 + 100 + 1 = 1201.

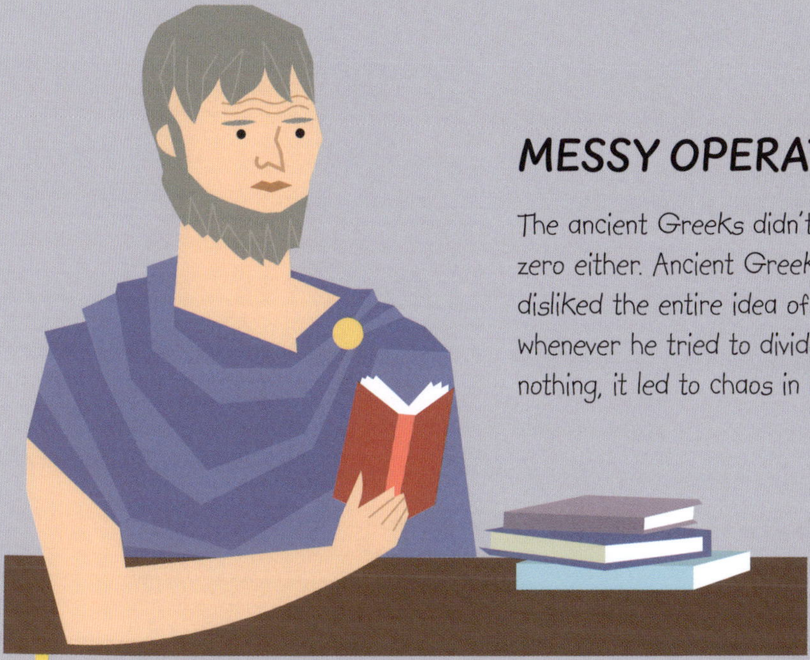

MESSY OPERATIONS

The ancient Greeks didn't have a number for zero either. Ancient Greek philosopher Aristotle disliked the entire idea of zero because whenever he tried to divide something by nothing, it led to chaos in his operations.

MAYAN SHELLS

The ancient Maya civilization of Central America used a shell to represent zero, but probably not as a number in its own right. It may have been a placeholder, similar to how the Babylonians left a space between numbers.

500 BCE

1st century BCE

628 CE

DID YOU KNOW?

Dividing by zero

It is impossible to divide by zero. To divide a quantity by zero is the same as arranging the quantity into equal groups of zero. But groups of zero only ever amount to zero.

RULES FOR ZERO

Indian mathematician Brahmagupta was the first person to treat zero as a number by coming up with rules about how to do operations with it:

When zero is added to a number, the number is unchanged.
When zero is subtracted, the number is unchanged.
A number multiplied by zero equals zero.
Zero divided by zero equals zero.

The first three rules are still considered true today, but we now know it is impossible to divide by zero.

SPREADING THE WORD

Muhammad al-Khwarizmi, who lived and worked in the city of Baghdad (in modern-day Iraq), wrote lots of books about math. He used the Hindu number system, which by now included zero as a number. His books were translated into many languages, which helped to spread the idea of zero as a number and numeral in its own right.

9th century

ZERO IN NORTH AFRICA

Arabic merchants traveling in North Africa spread the idea of zero among traders visiting from other parts of the world. Zero was quickly adopted by merchants from Europe, who were still using complicated Roman numerals at this time.

11th century

1202

ANGRY AT NOTHING

Having heard about zero while traveling in North Africa, Italian mathematician Fibonacci wrote about it in his book *Liber Abaci*. In doing so, he angered religious leaders, who associated zero or "nothingness" with evil. In 1299, zero was banned in Florence, Italy. The authorities were worried that it would encourage people to commit fraud, as 0 could easily be changed into a 9. But the number was so convenient that people continued to use it in secret.

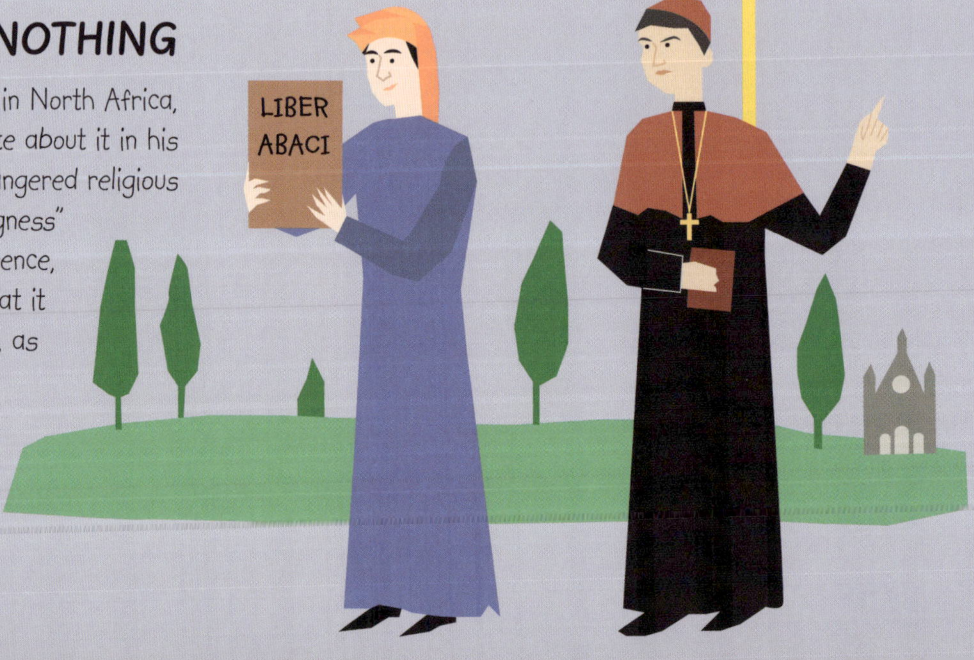

WRITING NOTHING

Meanwhile, a separate number system had developed in China. From around the 8th century, Chinese mathematicians left a space for zero, but by the 13th century, they started to use a round circle symbol.

COMPUTER SPEAK

All of today's computers, smartphones, and digital technology couldn't exist without zero. They use a system called binary code, which translates instructions into sequences made up of the numerals 0 and 1.

13th century

17th century

Today

NEW ADVANCES

By the 16th century, the Hindu-Arabic numeral system had finally been adopted across Europe and zero entered common use. Zero made it possible to carry out complex calculations that had previously been impossible using cumbersome Roman numerals, allowing mathematicians like Isaac Newton to make huge advances in their studies in the 17th century.

DID YOU KNOW?

Year zero

In the year 2000 CE, celebrations took place around the world to mark the start of the new millennium, but many people claim this was a year early. They think the new millennium really started on January 1, 2001 CE, because there was no year zero in the Common Era.

HOW TO BE NEGATIVE

The earliest known use of negative numbers dates back to ancient China, where merchants would use counting rods made of ivory or bamboo to keep track of their transactions and avoid running into debt. Red rods represented positive numbers and black ones were negative. We use the opposite color scheme today—if someone owes money, we say they are "in the red." Later, Indian mathematicians started using negative numbers, too, but they sometimes used the + symbol to signify them, also the opposite of what we do today.

2 The counting board developed into a "place value" system in which the position of the rods on the grid told you the value of the number.

3 A rod placed vertically represented 1, and numbers 2–5 were represented by the placement of additional vertical rods. A rod placed horizontally, joined onto the vertical rods, represented numbers 6–9.

Vertical numbers

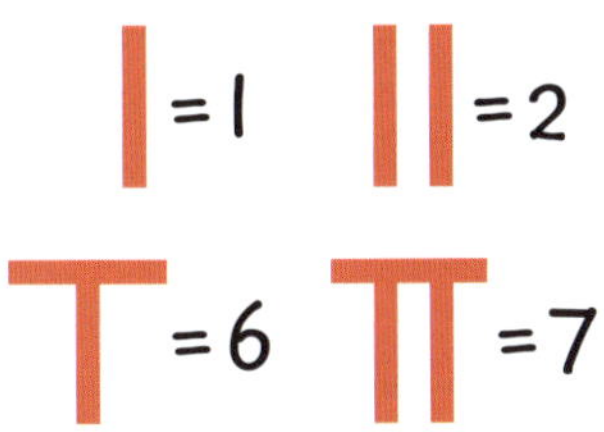

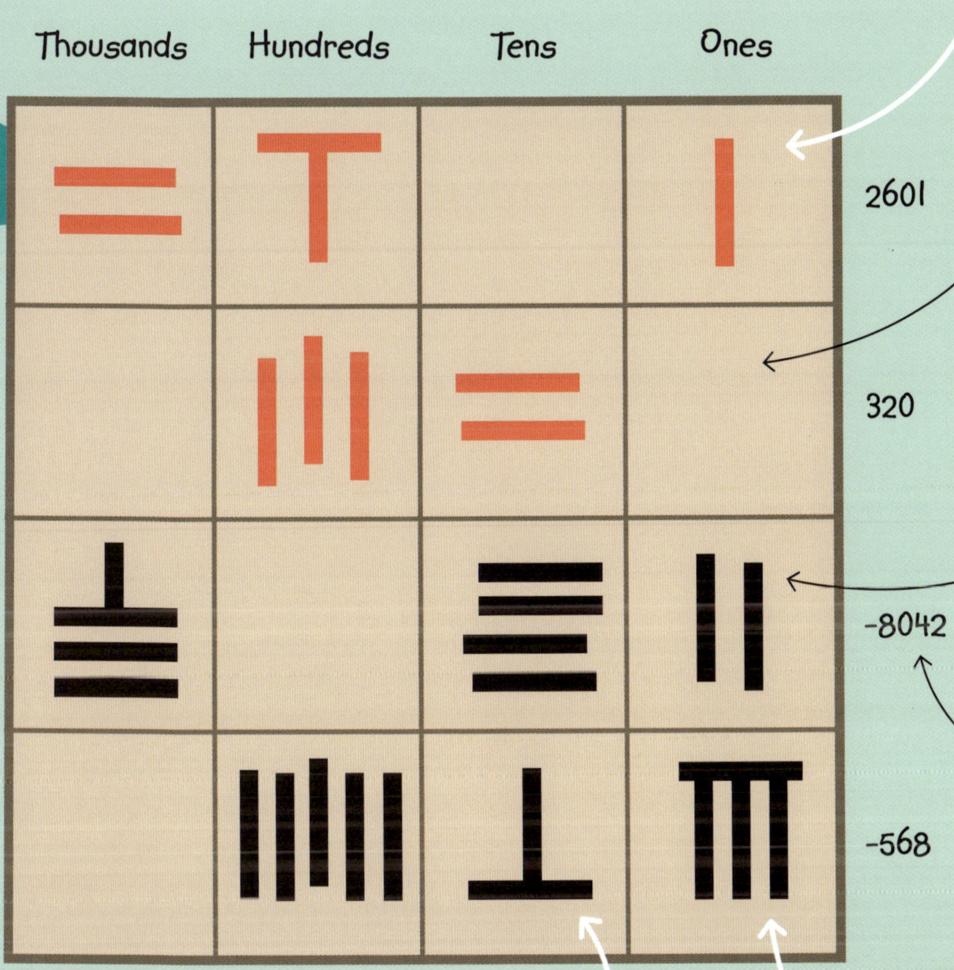

Before the invention of the 0 numeral, a blank space was left to represent zero.

The positional system works a lot like ours today. The two vertical rods in this column represents 2, but if they were in the hundreds column, they would represent 200.

The rods here represent the numbers 8 thousands, 0 hundreds, 4 tens, and 2 ones. The rods are black, so the number is negative. Therefore, the number represented is -8042.

4 Rods in the next column along (the "tens") were placed horizontally, with a vertical line joined onto the horizontal lines to represent numbers 6–9. In the next column (the "hundreds"), the rods would be placed vertically again. In this way, they would alternate along each row.

Horizontal numbers

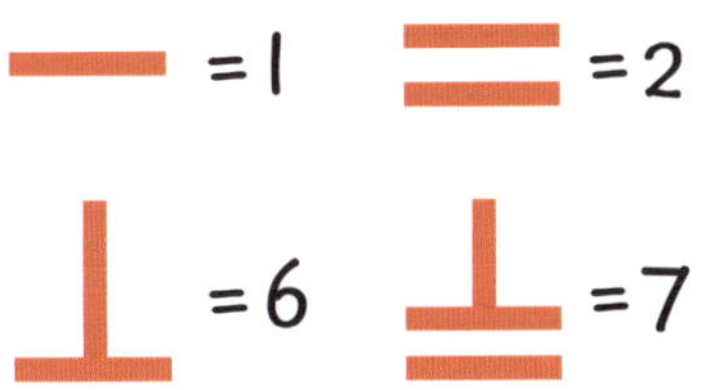

5 This system used red rods for positive numbers (money received) and black ones for negative numbers (money spent).

NEGATIVE NUMBERS

The easiest way to visualize how negative numbers work is to draw them out on a number line, with 0 in the middle. All the numbers to the right of 0 are positive, and all those to the left of 0 are negative. Today, negative numbers are represented with a - sign before the numeral.

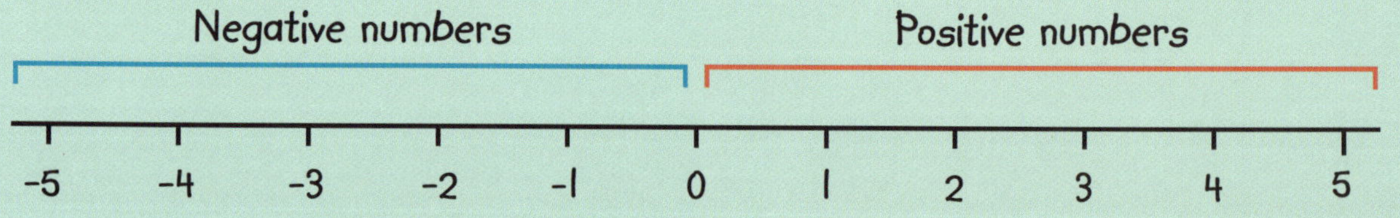

A - sign is always placed in front of negative numbers.

If a number has no sign, it is assumed to be positive.

ADDING POSITIVE AND NEGATIVE NUMBERS

When you add a positive number to any number, it causes that number to shift to the right along the number line. If you add a positive number to a smaller negative number, you will end up with a positive number. If you add a negative number to any number, it causes that number to shift to the left along the number line—this is the same as subtracting the equivalent positive number.

Adding a positive number moves it right along the number line.

$$(-2) + 3 = 1$$

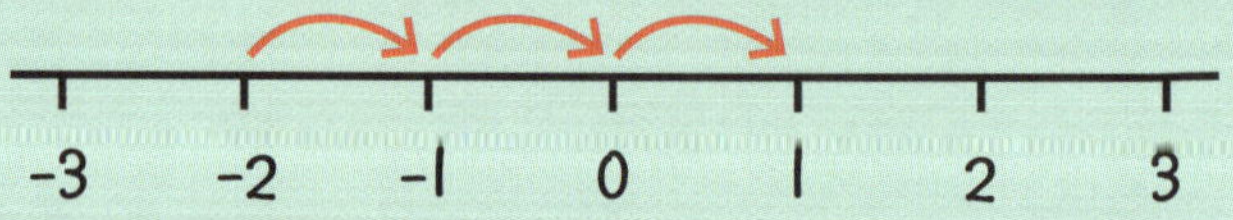

For calculations, often brackets are put around negative numbers to make them easier to read.

$$1 + (-2) = -1$$

$$1 - 2 = -1$$

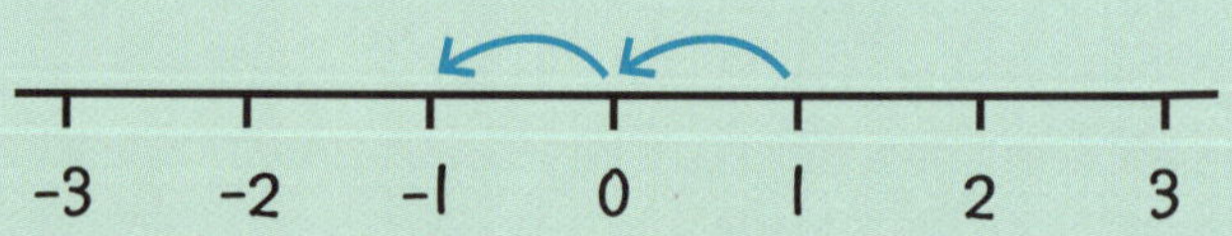

Adding a negative number to another number is the same as subtracting the equivalent positive number from that number.

SUBTRACTING POSITIVE AND NEGATIVE NUMBERS

If you subtract a positive number from a negative number, it works like normal subtracting, and you shift the number left along the number line. But if you subtract a negative number from a number (whether positive or negative), you create a "double negative"—the two minus signs cancel each other out, and you actually add the equivalent positive number onto the other number.

Subtracting a positive number from a negative number works like normal subtraction.

$$(-1) - 2 = -3$$

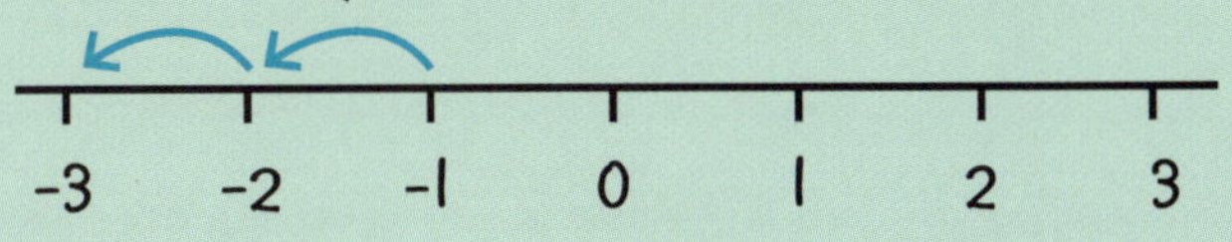

The two minus signs cancel each other out and create a positive.

$$(-2) - (-4) = 2$$

$$(-2) + 4 = 2$$

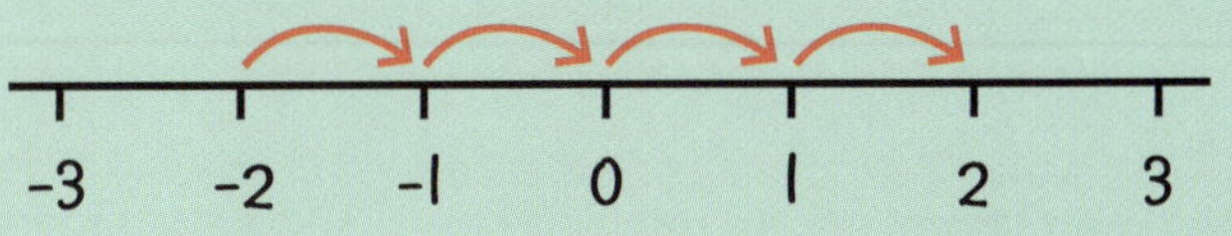

TRY IT OUT

EXTREME TEMPERATURES

Temperatures on Earth vary a lot. The hottest recorded surface temperature is 134°F (57°C) measured in Death Valley, California, on July 10, 1913. The coldest temperature ever recorded is -128°F (-89°C), measured at Vostok Station, Antarctica, on July 21, 1983.

What is the difference between the highest and lowest recorded temperatures?

The difference between two numbers is calculated by subtracting the smaller number from the larger one.

To find the answer in °F, you need to calculate 134 - (-128), and to find the answer in °C you need to calculate 57 - (-89). What's the difference between the hottest and coldest temperatures in each scale?

REAL WORLD

Sea levels

We use negative numbers to describe the height of places below sea level. Baku, in Azerbaijan, lies at 92 ft (28 m) below sea level, so we say it has an elevation of -92 ft (-28 m). It is the lowest-lying capital city on Earth.

HOW TO TAX YOUR CITIZENS

Percentages make it easy to compare amounts quickly—from supermarket discounts to battery charge levels. They have been used for raising taxes since ancient times. To raise money for the army of the ancient Roman Empire, every person who owned property had to pay tax. The tax officials agreed it wouldn't be fair to take the same amount from each individual, as the level of wealth varied from person to person. So they decided to take exactly one-hundredth, or 1 percent, from each person.

2 This person was pretty poor. He gave the tax official one-hundredth of his total amount of money.

1 The tax official found out how much money each person who owned property had and took one-hundredth of the total amount in tax.

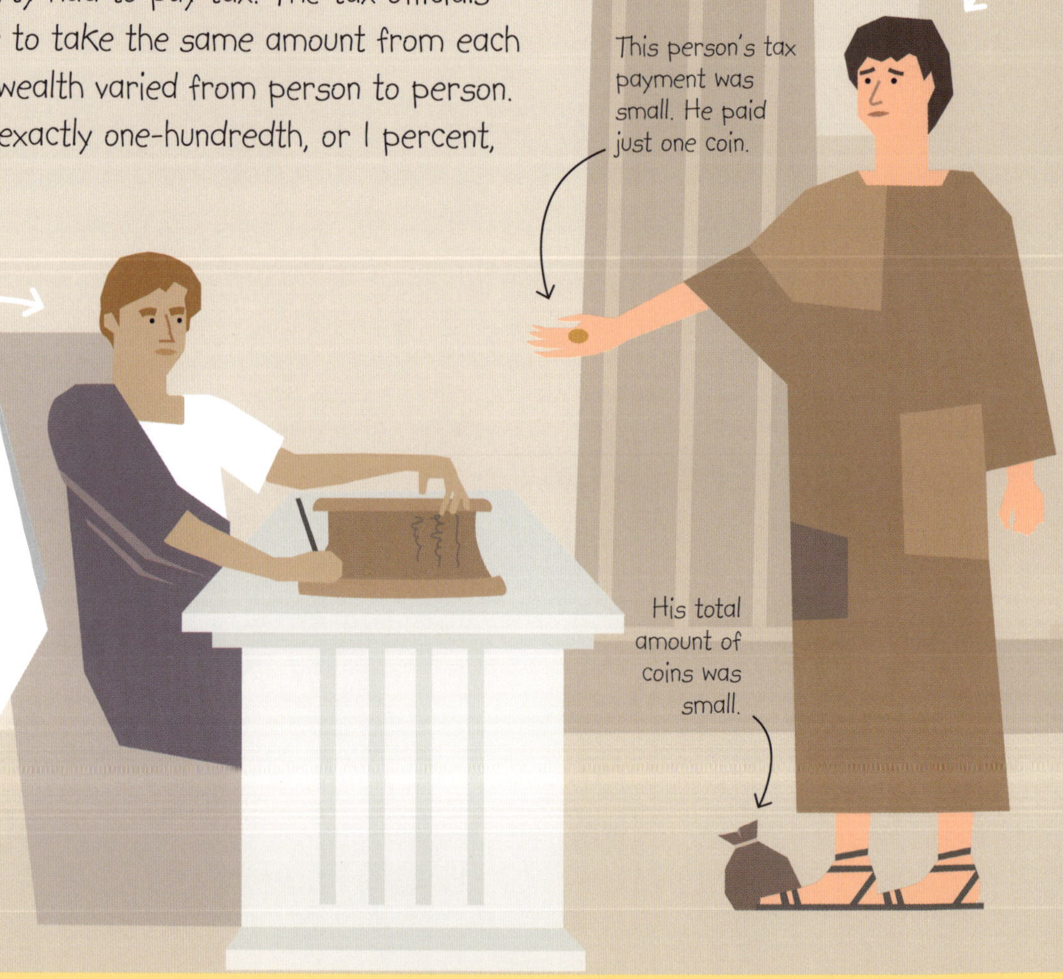

Doing the math
PERCENTAGES

A percentage is represented by the symbol % or the term "percent," which comes from the Latin language used by the Romans. It means "out of 100" or "per 100." If out of 100 coins, one is gold, we say that 1% of the coins is gold.

$\frac{1}{100}$ is equivalent to 1%

$\frac{75}{100}$ is equivalent to 75%

3 This person also gave one-hundredth of his money to the tax official, but it amounted to more coins than the first person, as he was richer.

4 An even richer person also gave the tax official one-hundredth of her money—the same percentage as everyone else. This was a much larger amount than both of the others but the same proportion of her overall wealth.

1% of 100 coins = 1 coin

1% of 3,000 coins = 30 coins

1% of 10,000 coins = 100 coins

To work out how much tax each person paid, you simply divide the total amount of coins they each had by 100 to find 1%. This was a fairer system than making everyone pay the same amount, as they all paid the same proportion of their wealth.

ALL IN PROPORTION

Suppose the emperor of Rome raises taxes of 250,000 coins in total. He wants to spend 20% on building new roads and the remaining 80% on equipment for his army. If he collects 250,000 coins in total, how many coins will he have to spend on building new roads and how many will be left for the army?

PUZZLE

If a game has been reduced in a sale by 25% and is currently on sale for \$24, how much did it cost originally?

First, divide 250,000 into 100 equal parts to find 1% of the total amount:
1% of 250000 = 250000 ÷ 100 = 2500

Then multiply 2,500 by the percentage you want to find—in this case, 20%:
2500 x 20 = 50000 coins
This is the amount he has to spend on building new roads.

Next, you need to subtract the 50,000 coins the emperor wants to spend on building new roads from his total amount of 250,000:
250000 - 50000 = 200000

The emperor has 200,000 coins left to spend on his army.

REVERSE PERCENTAGES

If the emperor decides to spend 40% of his collected tax on building a statue, and that amount is 16,000 coins, what is the original amount of tax he collected?

To find out the original amount, you need to find out what 1% was and then multiply that number by 100.

First, divide 16,000 by 40 to find 1% of the original amount:
16000 ÷ 40 = 400 coins

Then multiply that by 100:
400 x 100 = 40000 coins

The original amount of money the emperor collected in tax was 40,000 coins.

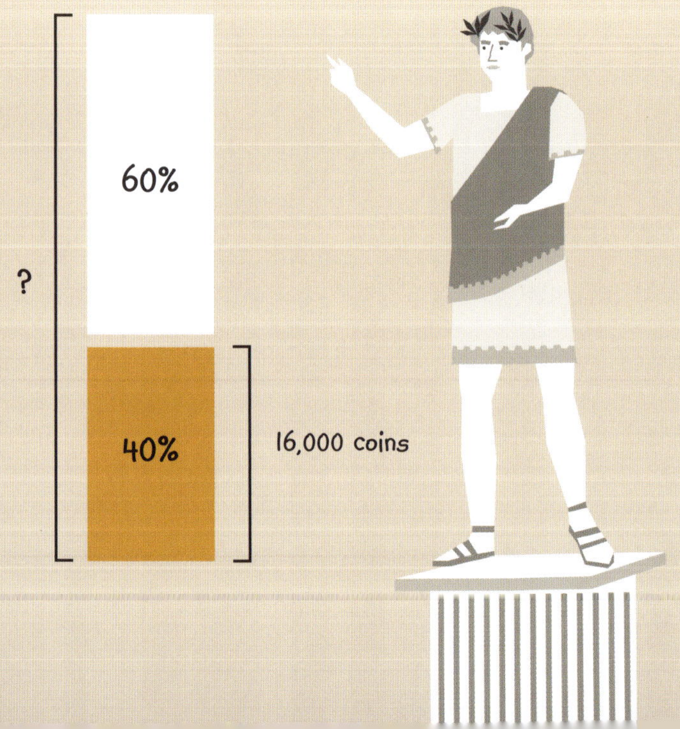

TRY IT OUT

HOW TO GET A BARGAIN

The best way to compare prices in a supermarket is to work out the unit price of each item, such as the price per ounce. A 17 oz tub of ice cream normally costs $3.90, but the supermarket has two special offers running. Which one is the better value—Deal A or Deal B?

To compare the two deals, you need to work out the unit price of the ice cream. The easiest way to do this is to find the price of 1 ounce in cents.

For Deal A:

The total amount of ice cream is 17 oz + 50% extra (8.5 oz) = 25.5 oz.

Unit price = total price ÷ number of ounces
= 390¢ ÷ 25.5 = **15¢ per ounce.**

For Deal B:

You need to work out the price of the 17 oz tub after 40% is taken off:

New price with 40% off = 60% of old price
= 0.6 x 390¢ = 234¢.

Then you can calculate the unit price:
Unit price = total price ÷ number of ounces
= 234¢ ÷ 17 = **14¢ per ounce.**

Of the two, Deal B is better—taking 40% off the original price of $3.90 is a better value than adding 50% more ice cream.

Next time you go shopping, try to spot any deals that appear better in value than they really are!

REAL WORLD

Sports achievements

Sports commentators sometimes use percentages to describe how successful players are. For example, in tennis, they often talk about the percentage of first serves that are "in." A high percentage of "in" serves means that the player is playing very well.

HOW TO USE PROPORTIONS

Fractions and decimals allow us to express and to simplify numbers that are not whole numbers. They are simply different ways of showing the same number. Whether you describe something using fractions or decimals depends on the situation.

FRACTIONS

If you want to talk about a part of a whole number, you can use a fraction. A fraction is made up of a denominator (the number of parts that the whole number has been split into) and a numerator (the number of parts that you are dealing with). If you imagine a pizza cut into just two even slices, each slice is $\frac{1}{2}$ of the pizza. If you cut it into three, each slice is $\frac{1}{3}$, and if you cut it into four, each slice is $\frac{1}{4}$.

DECIMALS

Imagine a 100-meter running race in which all four athletes crossed the line in a time of 10 seconds. You wouldn't know which of them had won! Decimals help you to be much more precise. If you knew that the runners crossed the line in 10.2, 10.4, 10.1, and 10.3 seconds, you'd be able to work out exactly who came in first, second, third, and fourth.

Decimals are written using a decimal point.

Tens	Ones	Decimal point	Tenths	Hundredths	Thousandths	Ten thousandths
1	0	.	7	8	4	9

Figures to the left of the decimal point represent whole numbers.

Figures to the right of the decimal point represent part of a whole number.

The whole number, 1, is represented by this single unbroken rectangle.

When the rectangle is split down the middle, it is made up of two halves, which can be written either as $^1/_2$ or 0.5.

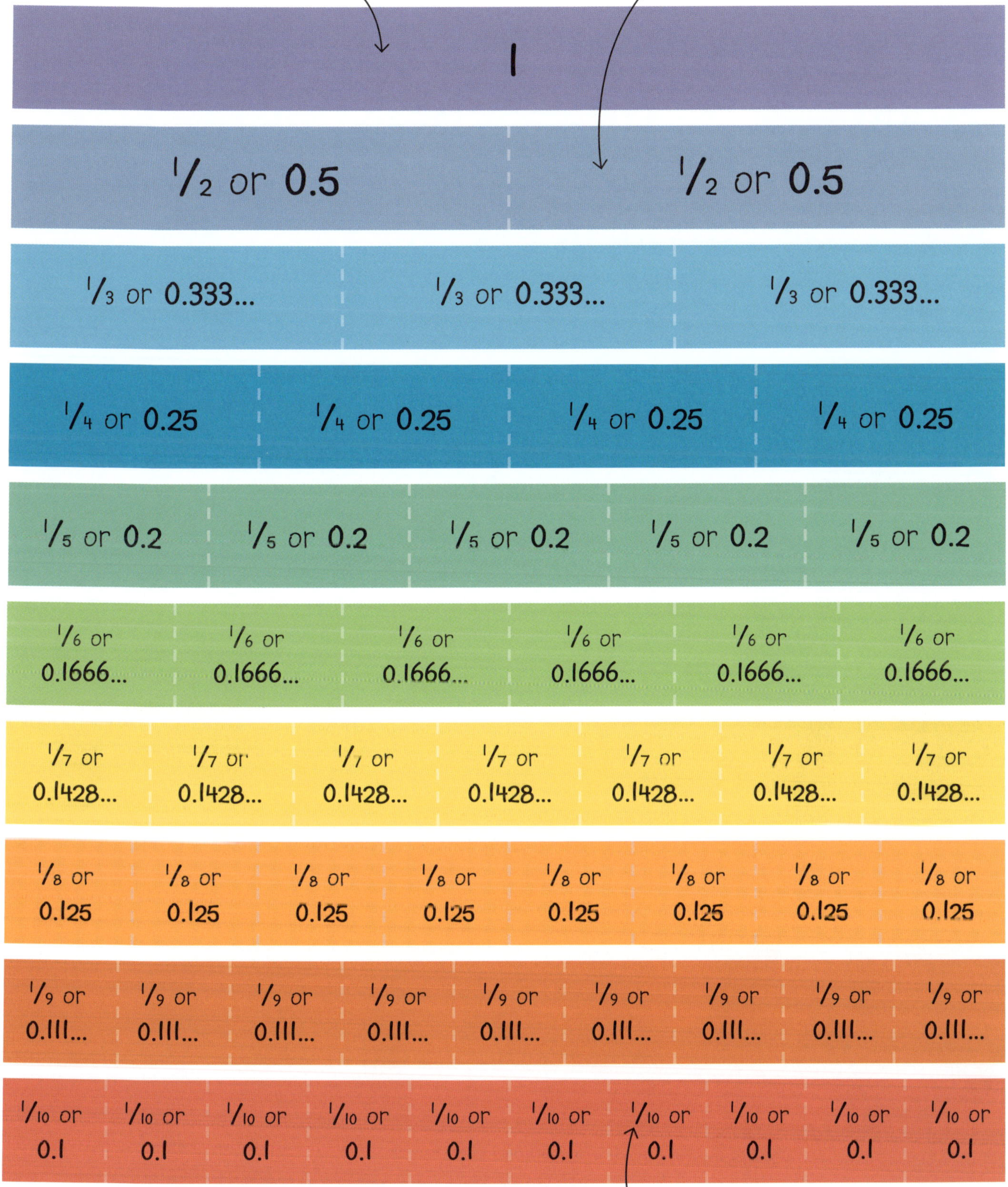

When the rectangle is split up into 10 even parts, each part represents $^1/_{10}$ of 1, or 0.1.

The dividing line in a fraction is called the vinculum.

HOW TO KNOW THE UNKNOWN

If there's something in a math problem that you don't know, algebra can help! Algebra is a part of math where you use letters and symbols to represent things that you don't know. You work out their values by using the things you do know and the rules of algebra. Thinking algebraically is a vital skill that's important in lots of subjects, such as engineering, physics, and computer science.

AL-JABR

Algebra is named after the Arabic word *al-jabr*, which means the "reunion of broken parts." This word appeared in the title of a book written around 820 CE by mathematician Muhammad al-Khwarizmi, who lived and worked in the city of Baghdad (in modern-day Iraq). His ideas led to a whole new branch of math that we now call "algebra."

MEASURING MEDICINE

To cure a patient, getting the right dosage of medicine is crucial. Algebra helps doctors to figure out the right dosage by assessing a patient's illness and general health, the effectiveness of different drugs, and any other factor that may affect their recovery.

PUZZLE

You have a package of candy. Your friend takes six pieces. You're left with a third of what you started with. How much candy did you start with?

ALGEBRA ON THE ROAD

Algebra has made it possible for computers and artificial intelligence (AI) to control vehicles without the need for drivers. A driverless car uses algebra to calculate exactly when it is safe to turn, brake, stop, and accelerate based on the information its computer records of the car's speed, direction, and immediate environment.

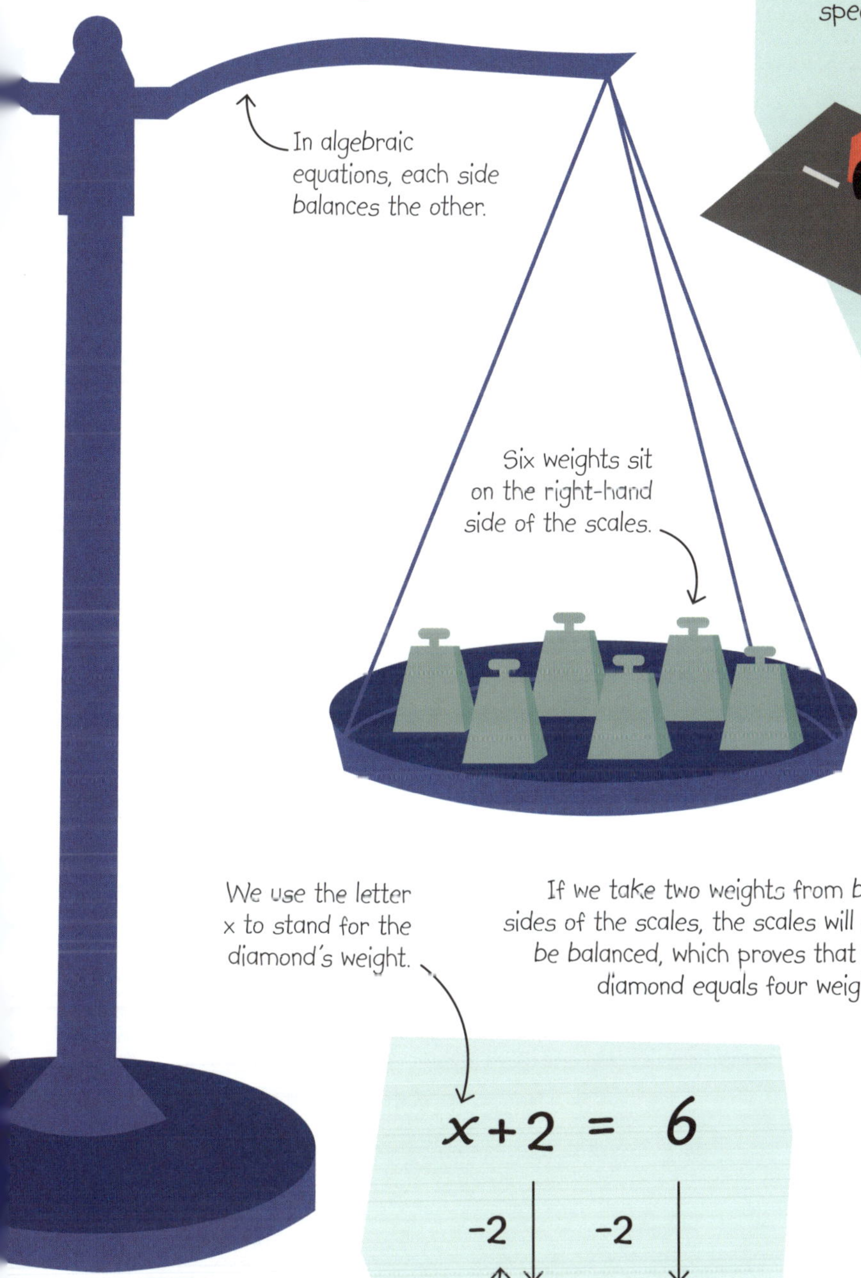

In algebraic equations, each side balances the other.

Six weights sit on the right-hand side of the scales.

BALANCING ACT

An algebraic equation can be seen as a set of scales. Whatever we do to one side, we must do to the other so the scales balance. In this example, we are trying to work out the weight of the diamond. We know that the diamond plus two weights equals six weights. Through algebra, we can prove that the diamond equals four weights.

We use the letter x to stand for the diamond's weight.

If we take two weights from both sides of the scales, the scales will still be balanced, which proves that the diamond equals four weights.

$$x + 2 = 6$$

$$-2 \qquad -2$$

$$x = 4$$

To find the weight of x on its own, we take two weights away from both sides of the equation.

In the end, we have used algebra to work out that x = 4.

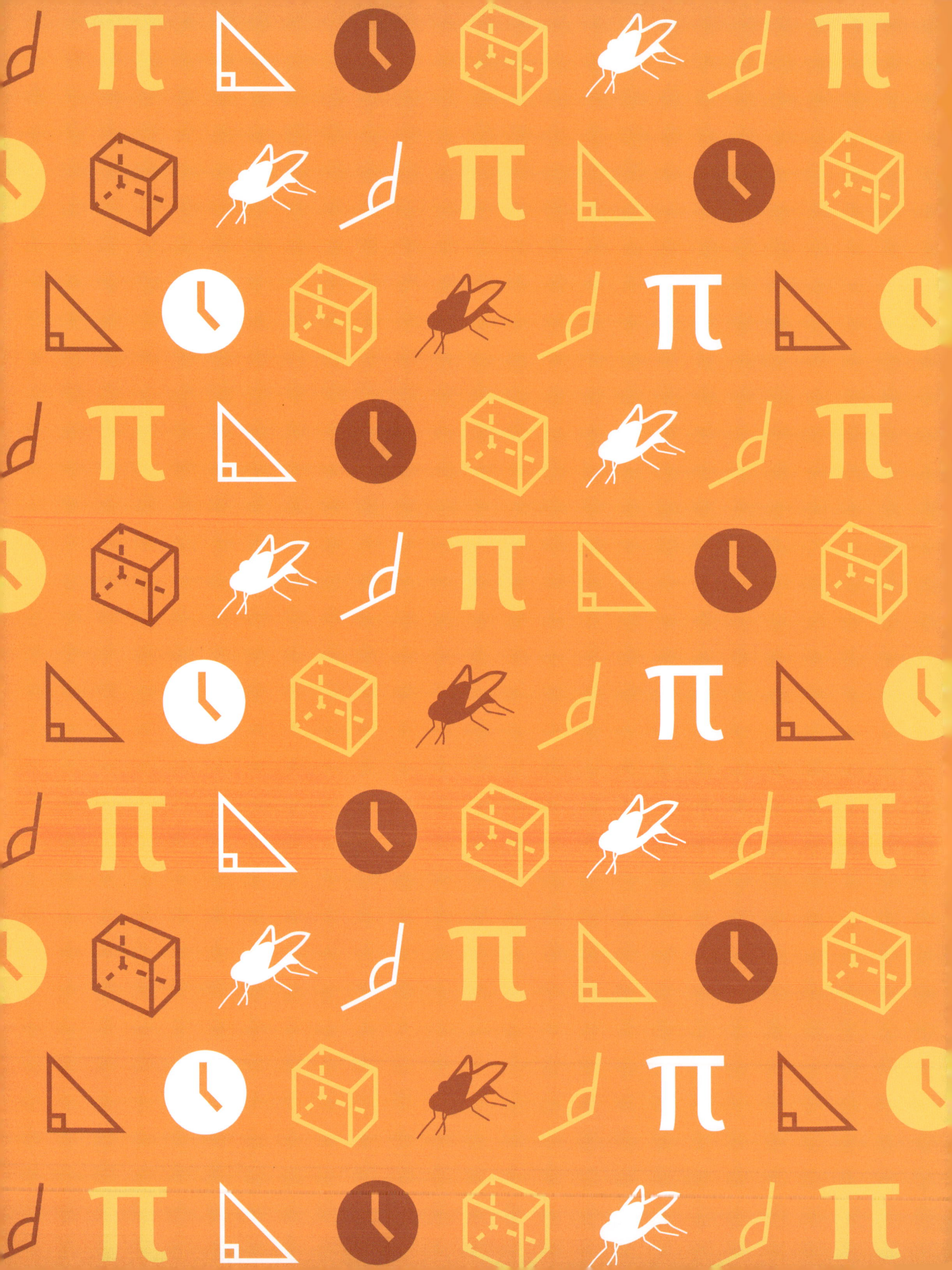

WHAT'S THE POINT OF

SHAPES AND MEASURING?

Making sense of the world around us would be impossible without geometry—the study of shapes, size, and space. Throughout history, our ways of measuring length, area, and volume, as well as time, have become much more precise. But ideas and theories about geometry first considered in ancient times are still in use today—in everything from finding locations using GPS navigation systems to building beautiful structures.

HOW TO SHAPE UP

Geometry—the study of shapes, size, and space—is one of the oldest topics in math. It was studied by the ancient Babylonians and Egyptians as long as 4,000 years ago. The Greek mathematician Euclid set out key geometric principles around 300 BCE. Geometry is an important part of fields as diverse as navigation, architecture, and astronomy.

BEE BUILDERS

Bees use a hexagonal honeycomb made of wax to house their developing larvae and to store honey and pollen. The hexagonal shape is ideal—the hexagons fit together perfectly, maximizing space while also using the least amount of wax. The overall shape is incredibly strong, as any movement within the honeycomb (such as the movement of the bees) or outside it (such as the wind) is spread evenly across the structure.

The bees create cylindrical cells, but their body heat causes the wax to melt and form hexagons.

Circle

A two-dimensional (2D) shape where each point of its circumference is the same distance, known as the radius, from the center.

Triangle

A 2D shape with three sides. The angles inside any triangle always add up to 180°, regardless of the lengths of the sides.

Square

A 2D shape with four sides of equal length and containing four 90° angles (also known as right angles).

Pentagon

A 2D shape with five sides. A regular pentagon has five sides of equal length, and each inside angle is 108°.

Sphere

A round, three-dimensional (3D) shape where every point on the surface is the same distance from the center.

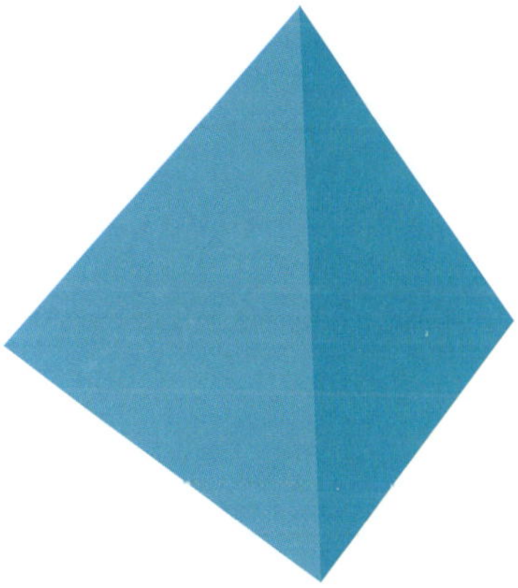

Pyramid

A 3D shape with triangular sides and a base that can be triangular, square, or another shape.

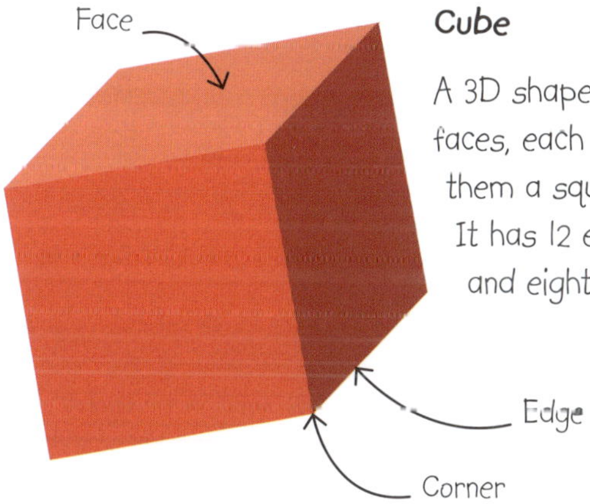

Cube

A 3D shape with six faces, each one of them a square. It has 12 edges and eight corners.

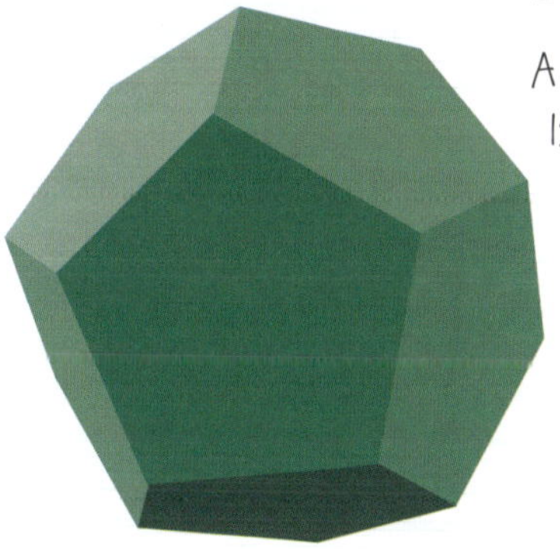

Dodecahedron

A 3D shape with 12 faces (each one of them a pentagon with equal sides), 30 edges, and 20 corners.

THE RIGHT SHAPE

Geometry helps us find shapes that are perfect for the job they are expected to do. Imagine trying to play soccer with a cube-shaped ball—it would be hard to kick and pass! Whether something has been designed by humans or evolved in the natural world, the shapes of the things around us either are set and as good as they will ever be or are constantly being improved.

PRETTY PATTERNS

When shapes are combined and repeated in a pattern without gaps or overlapping, it is called "tessellation." Tessellation can be decorative, such as in a mosaic, or it can be practical, such as the way bricks are overlapped to increase a wall's stability.

REFLECTIVE SYMMETRY

A shape has reflective symmetry if a straight line can split it into two halves that are perfect reflections of each other. The line is called a line of symmetry. A 3D shape has reflective symmetry if a plane can split it into halves that reflect each other. Symmetrical shapes can have one or more of these lines or planes.

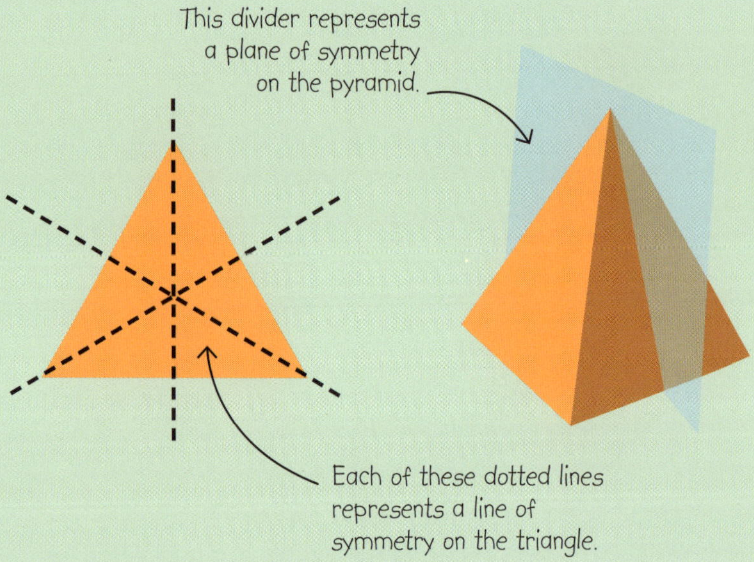

HOW TO USE SYMMETRY

If a two-dimensional (2D) shape or three-dimensional (3D) object can be divided into two or more identical pieces, we say it has symmetry. Symmetry can be seen everywhere in nature, from the petals of a flower to the frozen water molecules of a snowflake. The simplicity and order of symmetry make it visually appealing, so artists, designers, and architects regularly use it as inspiration for elements of their creations.

SYMMETRY IN ARCHITECTURE

Architects often want to make their buildings as symmetrical as possible. The Taj Mahal in India is perfectly symmetrical from the front and also if you look at it from above. The four large towers that surround it, called minarets, emphasize this symmetry.

ROTATIONAL SYMMETRY

Rotational symmetry occurs when a shape can be rotated around a fixed point and still appear the same. For a 2D shape, the rotation is around a center of rotation, and for a 3D shape, it is around an axis. The number of times that the shape appears the same when rotated 360° is called its order of rotation.

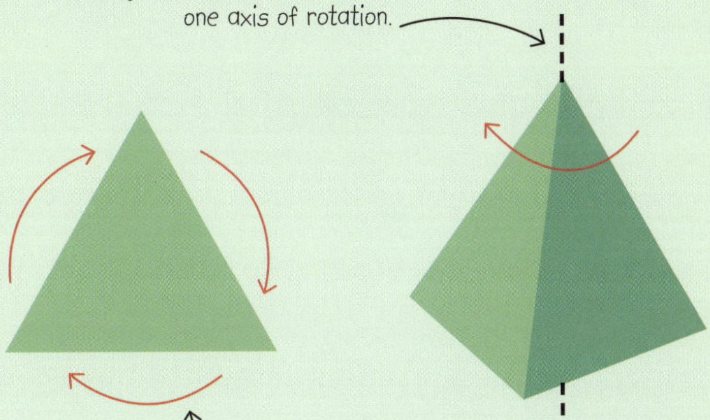

SYMMETRY IN NATURE

Nature is full of symmetry—even humans are almost symmetrical. When water molecules freeze into snowflakes, they form ice crystals with hexagonal symmetry. Starfish have an order of rotation of five, which allows them to move in many directions, easily find food, or swim away if threatened. Fiddler crabs are asymmetrical—they have no planes of symmetry at all.

DID YOU KNOW?

Infinite symmetry

Circles and spheres have an infinite amount of both reflective and rotational symmetry—they are perfectly symmetrical shapes.

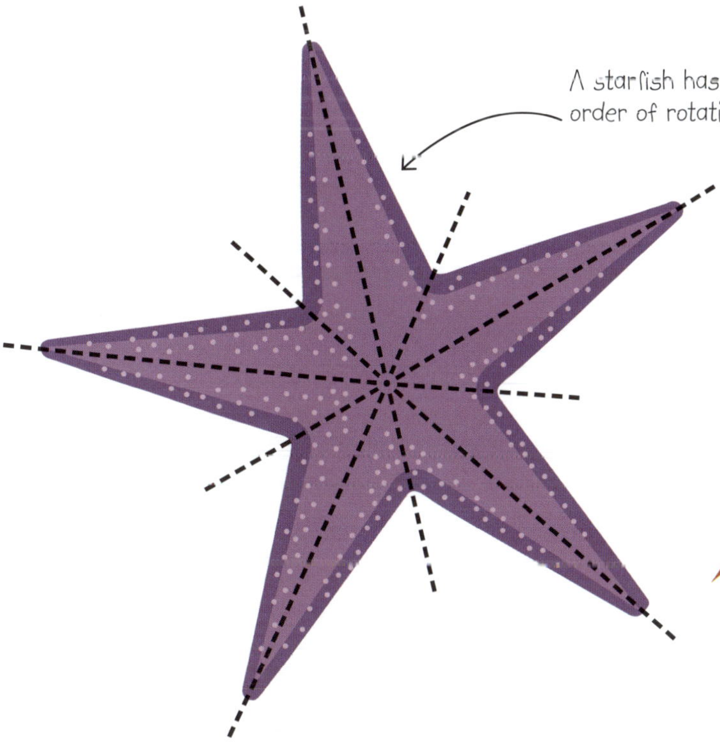

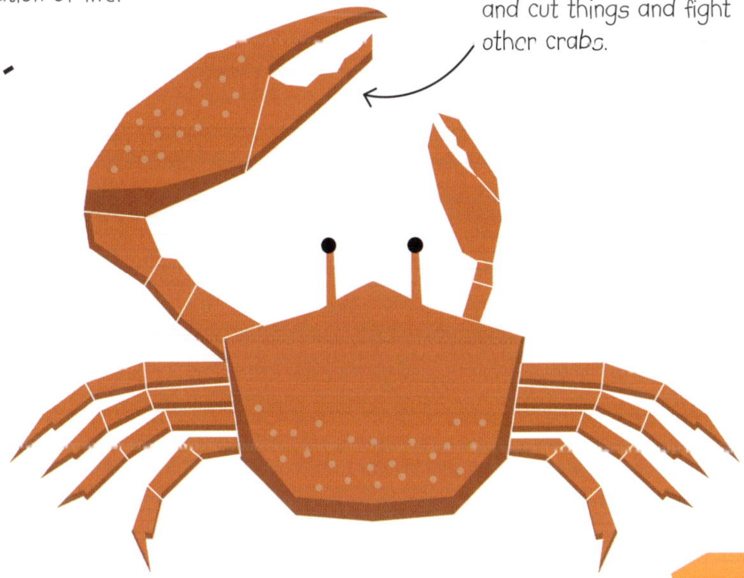

HOW TO MEASURE A PYRAMID

How can you measure the height of something if you can't reach the top with a tape measure? The answer is to use right-angled triangles—a trick discovered thousands of years ago. Built with more than 2.3 million blocks of stone, the Great Pyramid in Egypt is enormous. When the ancient Greek mathematician Thales visited in about 600 BCE, he asked the Egyptian priests exactly how tall it was, but they wouldn't tell him. So he decided to figure it out it for himself.

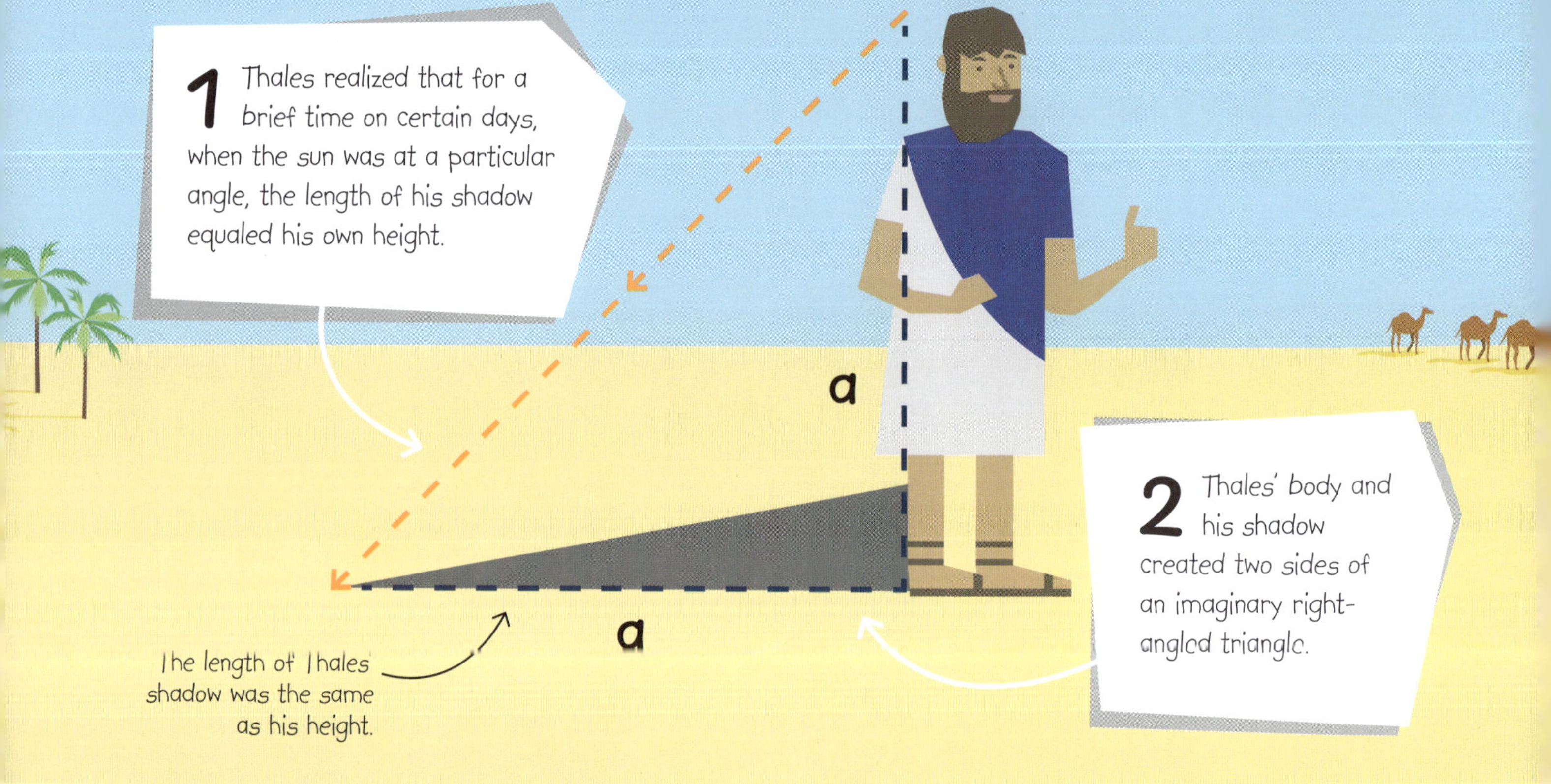

Doing the math
RIGHT-ANGLED TRIANGLES

Thales' measurements worked because the angle of the sun, his body, and his shadow formed an imaginary right-angled triangle. In these types of triangle, one corner is 90° (a right angle) and the other two corners add up to 90°. If two angles of a triangle are equal, then two sides must be equal, too.

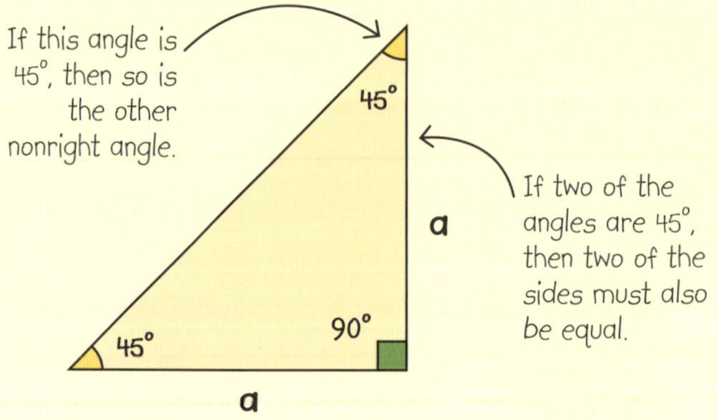

3 Thales realized that at that time of day, everything else—including the Great Pyramid—would also cast a shadow forming part of its own imaginary triangle. The height of the pyramid was one side of this imaginary triangle, and another was the length of the shadow, plus half of its base.

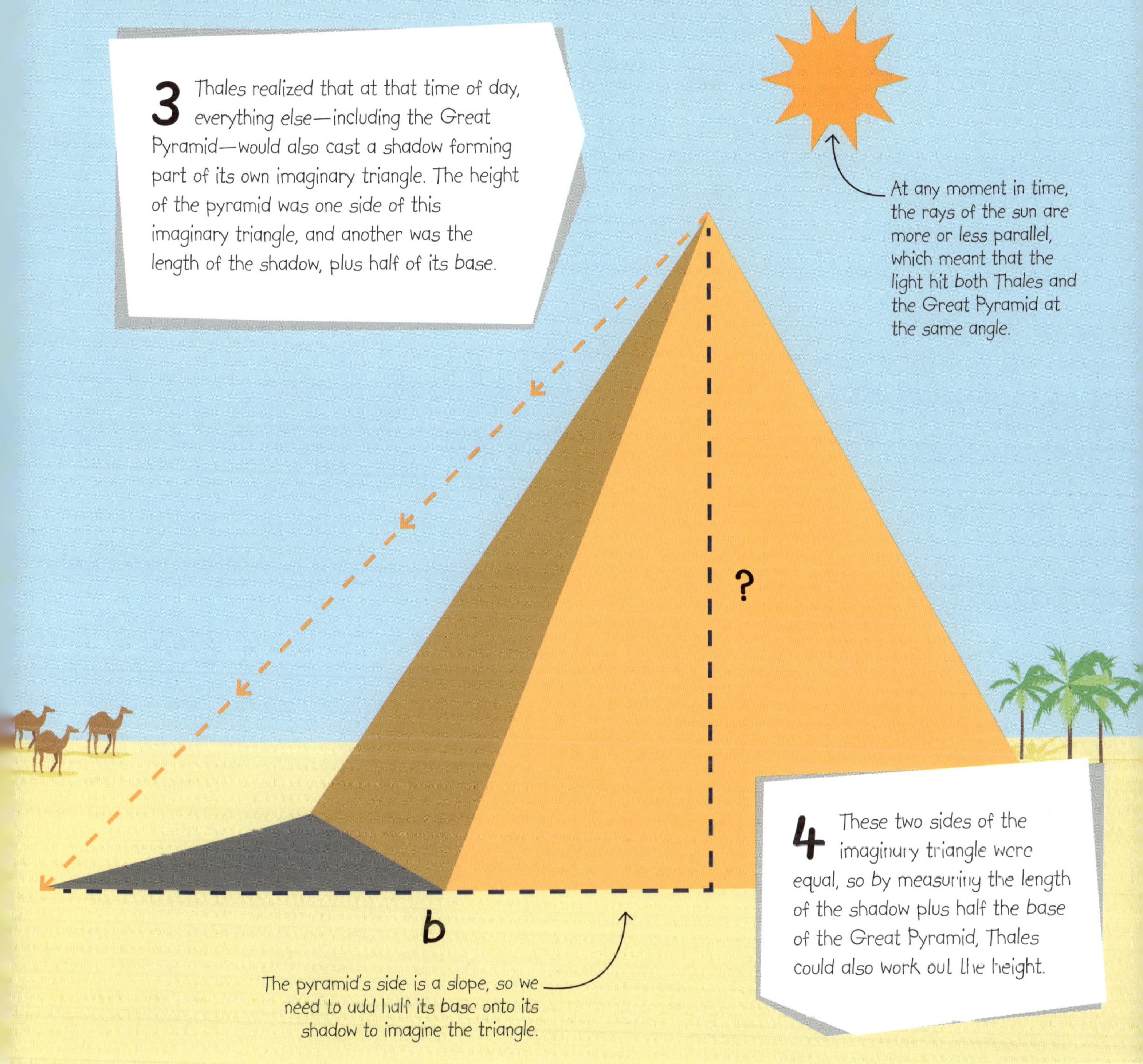

4 These two sides of the imaginary triangle were equal, so by measuring the length of the shadow plus half the base of the Great Pyramid, Thales could also work out the height.

When the Sun shone at 45°, creating the third side of the triangle, Thales knew that the other two sides would be of equal length (a). His shadow would be as long as he was tall. Thales also knew the pyramid would behave in the same way, so he paced out the pyramid's shadow (plus half its base) to measure it. This came to 481 ft (146.5 m), so the pyramid was 481 ft (146.5 m) tall.

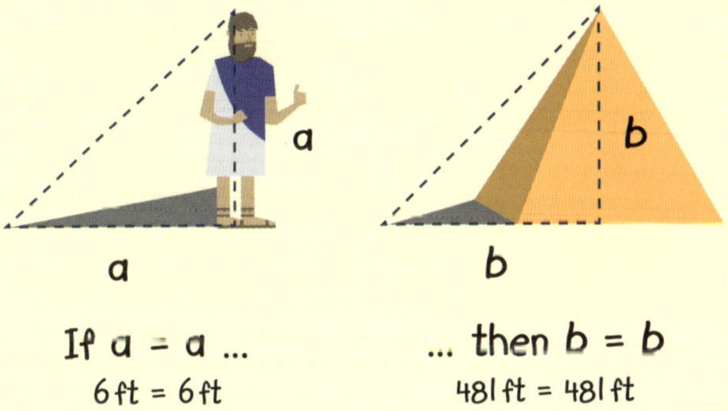

SIMILAR TRIANGLES

Later, another Greek mathematician, Hipparchus, developed Thales' idea further. He realized it was possible to measure objects using triangles with slopes of any angle—not just 45°. If Hipparchus had visited the Great Pyramid, he could have measured its height at any time of day by comparing its shadow to his own. Both shadows would have formed "similar triangles" – triangles that have exactly the same angles and proportions but are different in size.

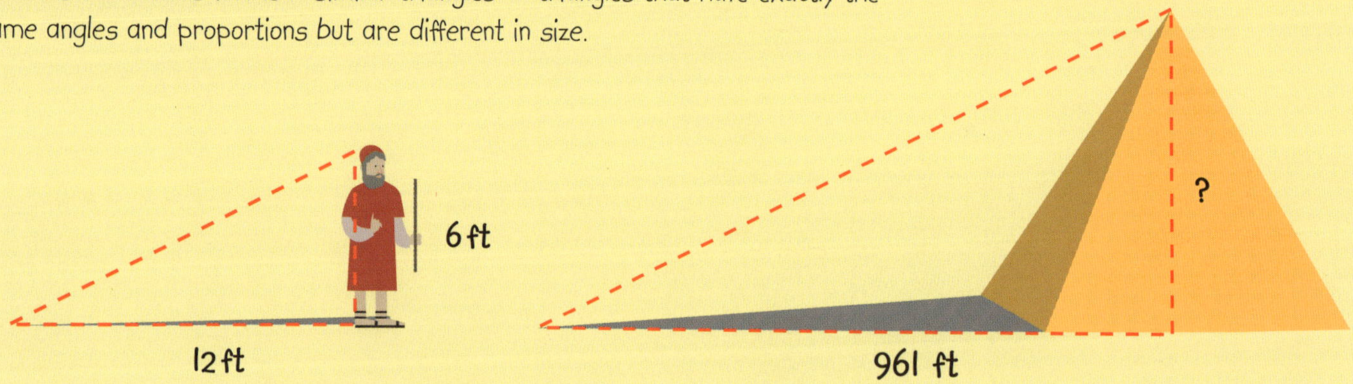

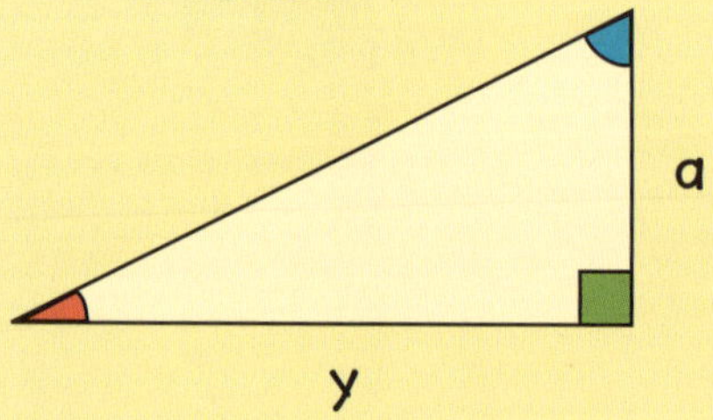

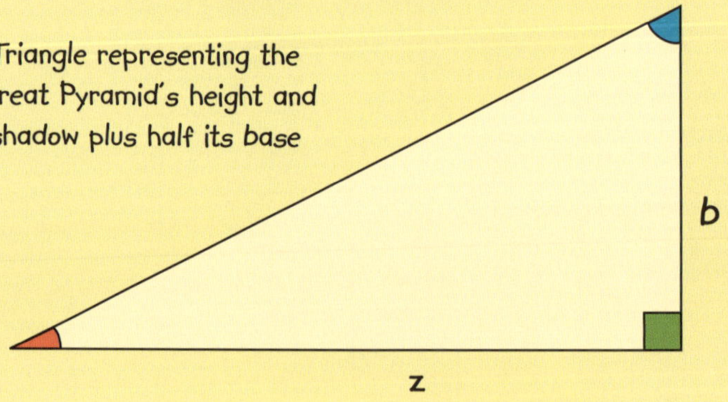

Because the imaginary triangles created by Hipparchus and by the pyramid are similar, knowing the height of one allows us to work out the height of the other.

We can work out the pyramid's height using a formula. The formula shows that Hipparchus's height (a) divided by his shadow (y) is the same as the Great Pyramid's height (b) divided by its shadow plus half the base (z) at the exact same time of day.

This is the unknown height of the pyramid.

This is Hipparchus's height.

$$\frac{a}{y} = \frac{b}{z}$$

This is the pyramid's shadow plus half its base.

This is Hipparchus's shadow.

This formula can be rearranged to work out the unknown measurement, b (the pyramid's height). To work out b, you need to divide a (person's height) by y (their shadow), then multiply by z (the pyramid's shadow plus half its base).

$$\frac{a}{y} \times z = b$$

$$\frac{6}{12} \times 961 = 480.5 \text{ ft}$$

This is the height of the pyramid.

REAL WORLD

Phone triangulation

Triangles are still used today to measure distances. Your smartphone's location can be pinpointed using "triangulation." A cell tower can tell how far away your phone is from it, but not exactly where you are. But if three different phone towers know how far away you are and each one draws a radius of that distance, the overlap between the three circles will pinpoint your location.

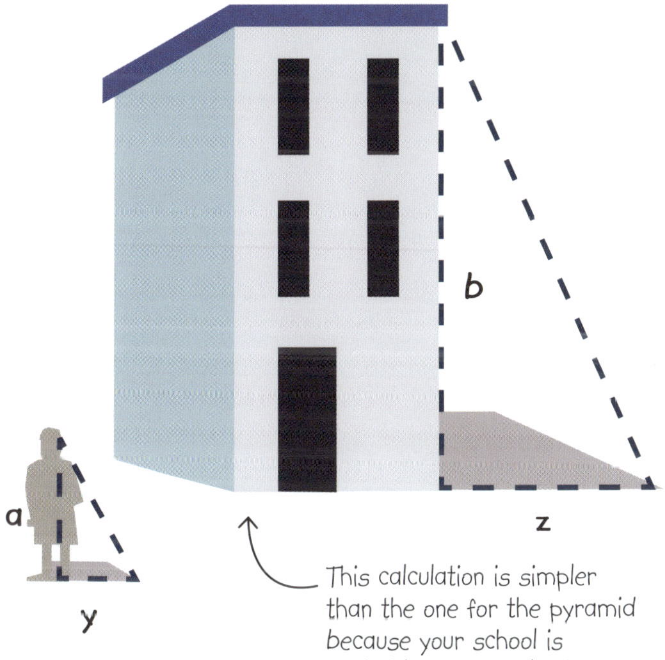

This calculation is simpler than the one for the pyramid because your school is probably a rectangle shape.

TRY IT OUT

MEASURE YOUR SCHOOL

On a bright, sunny day, your school building casts a 13 ft (4 m) shadow, and you cast a 20 in (0.5 m) shadow. If you're 4 ft 11 in (1.5 m) tall (or 59 in), how tall is your school?

Put these numbers into the formula.

$$b = \frac{a}{y} \times z = \frac{59}{20} \times 13 = 38\text{ ft}$$

So the building is around 38 ft (12 m) tall.

Now, if the sun is shining, why not try measuring the height of your home?

DID YOU KNOW?

Measuring with triangles

Hipparchus was a brilliant geographer, astronomer, and mathematician. He is called the "Father of trigonometry," a branch of math that studies how triangles can be used to measure things. Today, we use trigonometry in everything from designing buildings to space travel.

HOW TO MEASURE YOUR FIELD

Every year in Ancient Egypt, when the Nile River flooded, farmers' land boundaries were washed away. Afterward, they needed to find a way to make sure each farmer was given the same amount of land they had before the flood—but how could they measure this?

1 The Nile was central to ancient Egyptian life. Each flood carried mineral-rich silt that improved the farmers' soil but made working out who owned what very difficult.

Doing the math

FINDING THE AREA

By pulling the rope into a right-angled triangle, the ancient Egyptians could measure out bits of land. This helped them to be precise with their measurements.

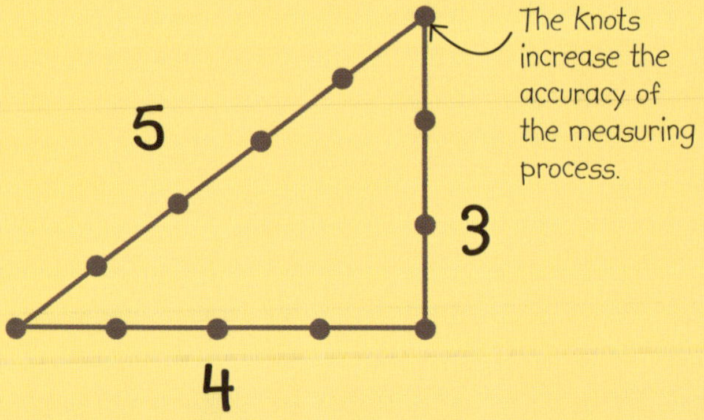

2 They realized that they could use a rope to work out each farmer's land area. By tying knots in the rope at regular lengths, they could use it a bit like a ruler.

3 Three people would pull the rope into the shape of a right-angled triangle. They then measured how many triangles were in a farmer's land and noted the answer for measuring again after the flood.

The triangle was right-angled, with three lengths on one side, another with four, and five on the remaining side.

The ancient Egyptians knew that to find the area of the triangle, they needed to multiply the height by the base and divide it by 2. So if each length was 1 unit, then:

$$\textbf{triangle area} = \frac{3 \times 4}{2} = 6 \text{ units}^2$$

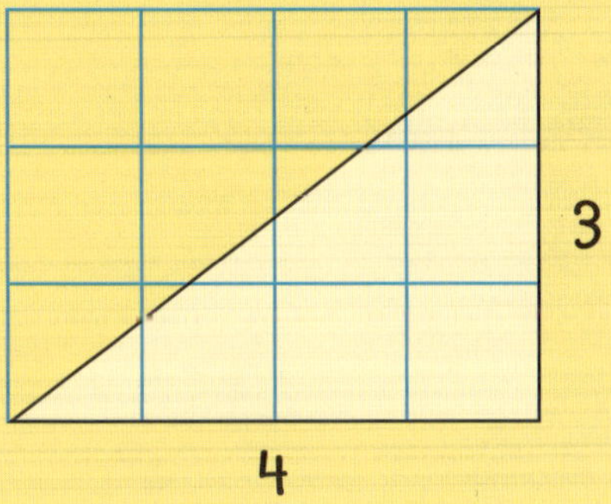

They could then patchwork as many triangles together as necessary to map out what each farmer had owned before the floods, knowing that each triangle was 6 units^2.

TRIANGLES AND RECTANGLES

A rectangle's area is calculated by multiplying its height by its base. A triangle with the same height and base will be exactly half that area.

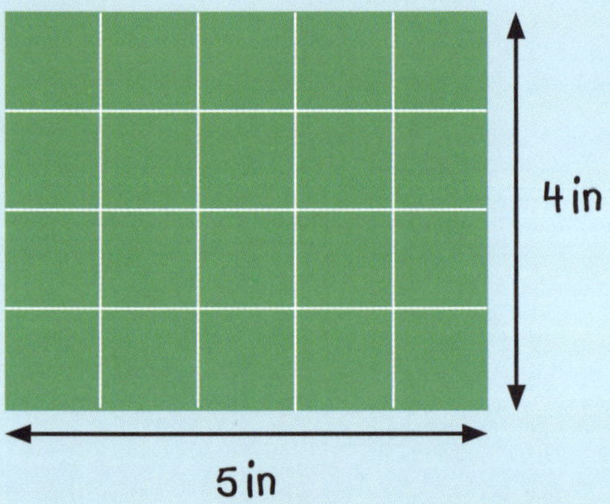

rectangle area = height × base

$$4 \times 5 = 20 \text{ in}^2$$

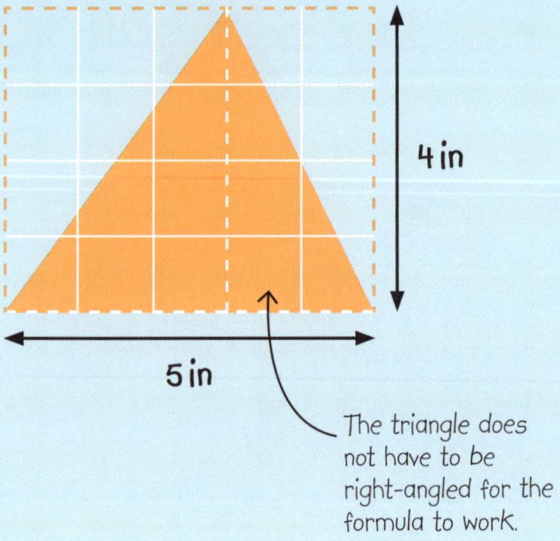

$$\text{triangle area} = \frac{(\text{height} \times \text{base})}{2}$$

$$\frac{4 \times 5}{2} = 10 \text{ in}^2$$

PARALLELOGRAMS

A parallelogram is any four-sided shape with two pairs of parallel sides. To work out a parallelogram's area, you need to multiply the height by the base, just as for a rectangle or square.

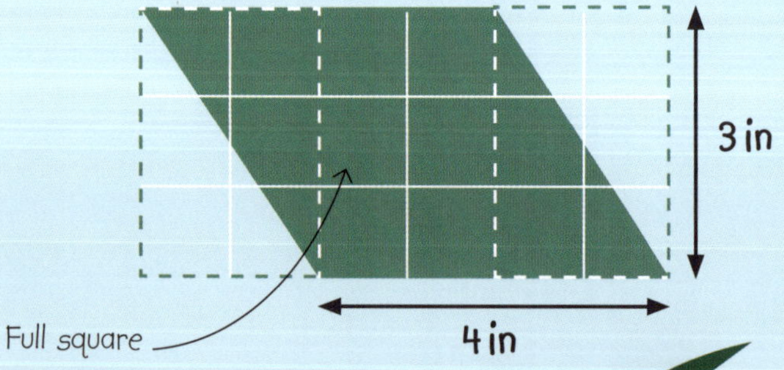

parallelogram area = (height × base)

$$3 \times 4 = 12 \text{ in}^2$$

ESTIMATING IRREGULAR SHAPES

What do you do if you need to work out the area of a shape more complicated than a triangle or rectangle? If it has straight sides, you can split it into right-angled triangles and work out each of their areas and add them together, as the people of Ancient Egypt did. If it has irregular sides, you can roughly estimate the area by drawing a regular shape of about the same size over it and counting its parts.

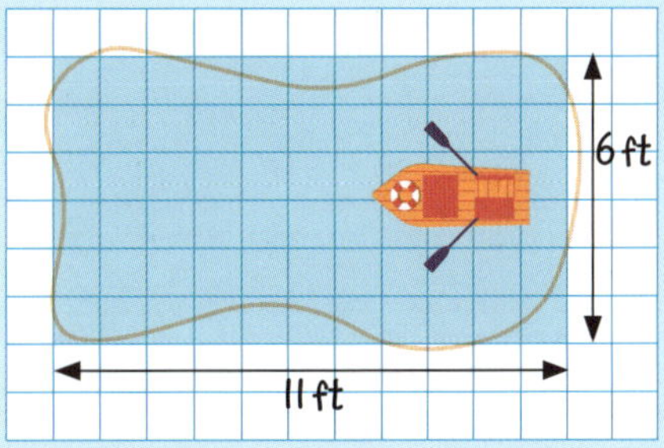

Area = 6 × 11
= 66 ft^2

To make a more accurate estimate, count all of the whole squares and halve any squares that are only partly full.

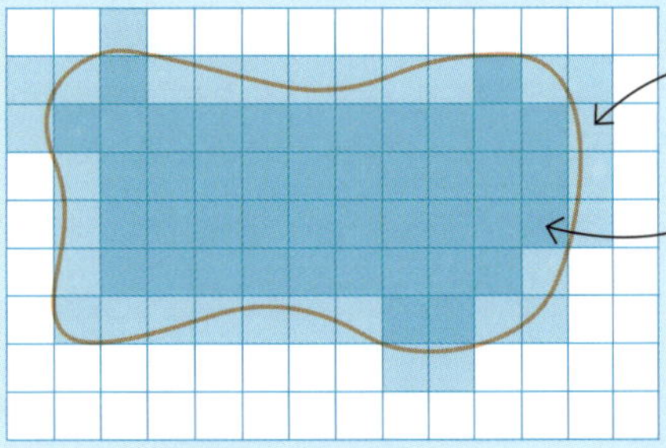

Partial square (31 in total)

Full square (44 in total)

Area = 44 + (31 ÷ 2)
= 59.5 ft^2

TRY IT OUT

AREA OF A ROOM

You need to work out how much it will cost to carpet a large room that's an awkward shape. The dimensions are shown to the right. Work out how much the carpet will cost if 1 square foot of carpet costs $20.

Divide up the area into simpler shapes and then work out the area of each.

Green triangle	= 3 × 2 × ½	= 3
Yellow triangle	= 2 × 2 × ½	= 2
Orange rectangle	= 5 × 6	= 30
Blue rectangle	= 6 × 4	= 24
Pink square	= 2 × 2	= 4
Total area		**= 63 ft^2**
Total cost	= 63 ft^2 × $20	**= $1260**

Now measure the area of your bedroom. Work out how much it would cost to re-carpet it, based on the same cost per square metre of carpet.

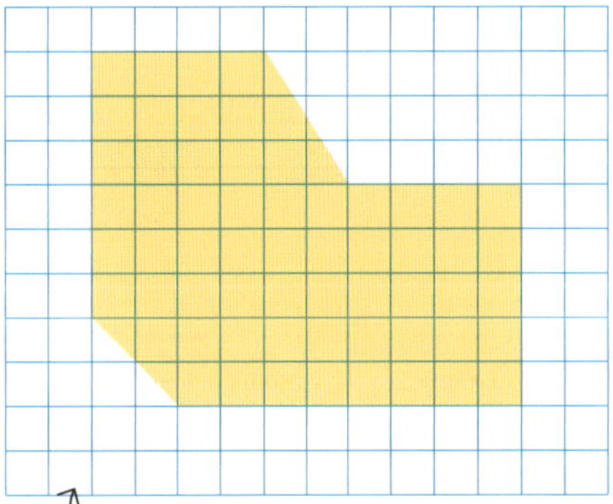

Each square is 1 ft^2.

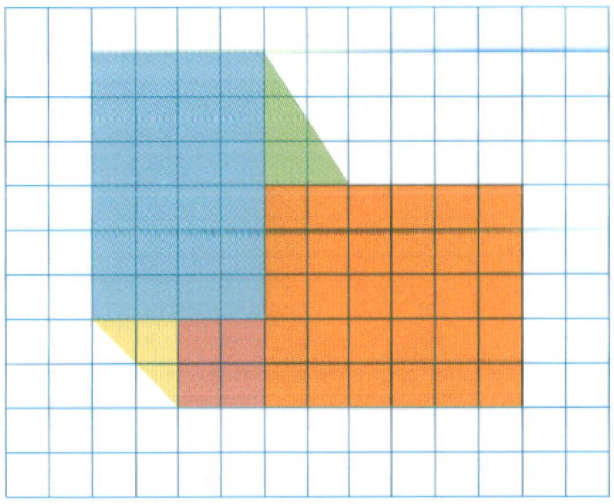

HOW TO MEASURE THE EARTH

Around 240 BCE, a scholar named Eratosthenes read a story about the sun's reflection on the water at the bottom of a well that happened just once a year. He started to think about how, at any one point in time, the sun's rays hit different parts of the world at different angles. He realized that with just two key pieces of information, he could estimate Earth's circumference. Amazingly, thousands of years before today's high-tech tools were invented, he estimated Earth's size with surprising accuracy.

1 The brilliant mathematician and scholar Eratosthenes was also head of the famous library of Alexandria in Egypt. One day, he read about a strange event in the south of the kingdom that happened for just a brief moment each year.

2 At noon on the longest day, in the town of Syene, the sun shone directly onto the water at the bottom of a deep well, which then reflected the light straight back up. At that moment, the sun was directly overhead.

3 This got Eratosthenes thinking. Was the sun ever exactly overhead back home in Alexandria? On the longest day, he found a tall pillar and waited for noon. The pillar cast a slight shadow, meaning that the light hit the ground at an angle.

He measured the pillar's height and the length of the shadow. By drawing a triangle, he worked out that the angle of the Sun's rays was 7.2°.

Eratosthenes knew that Earth was round, not flat, and realized that this was the cause of the difference in angles. He just needed one more piece of information ...

Eratosthenes knew that the sun hit Earth in parallel rays because it was so far away.

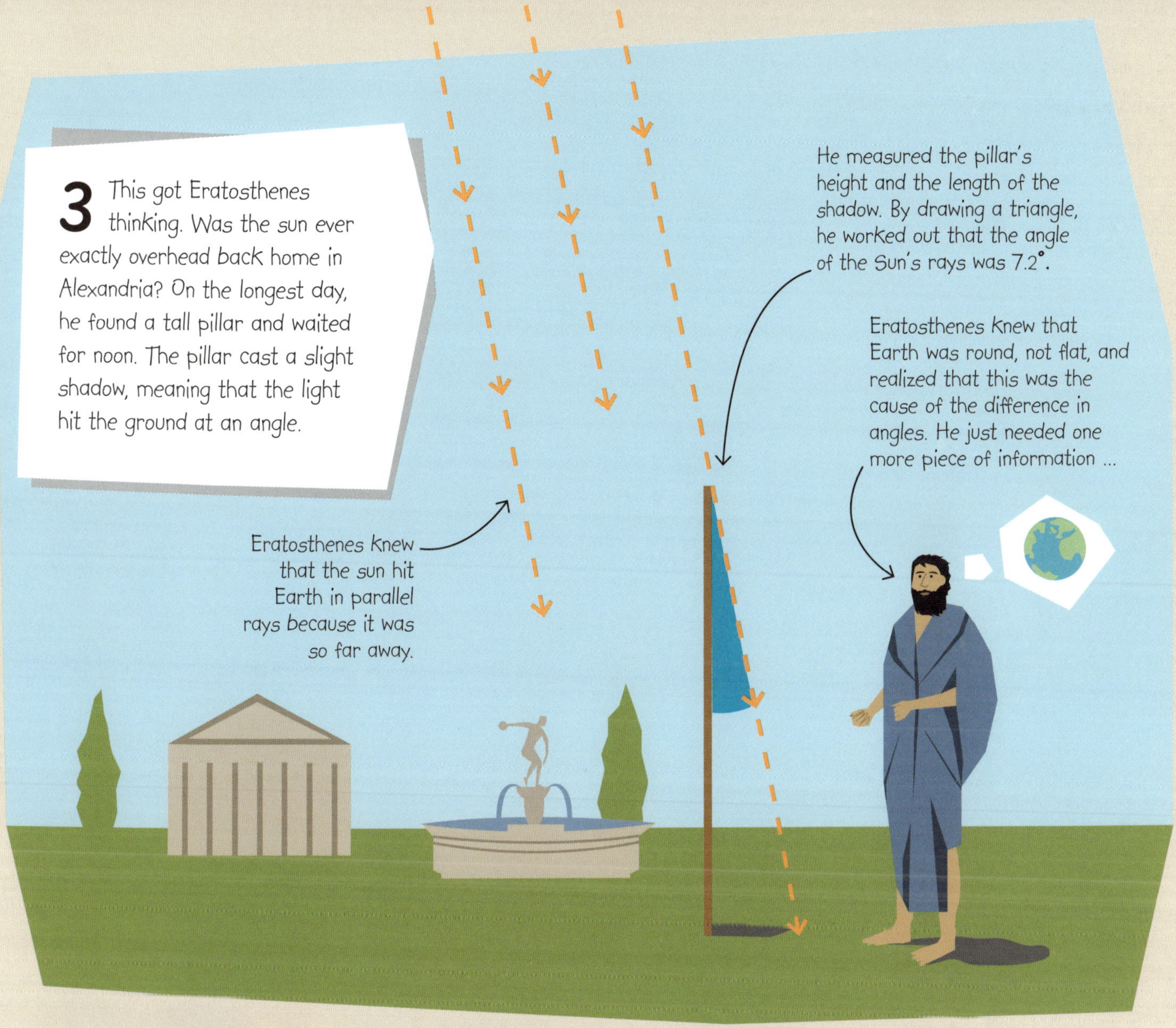

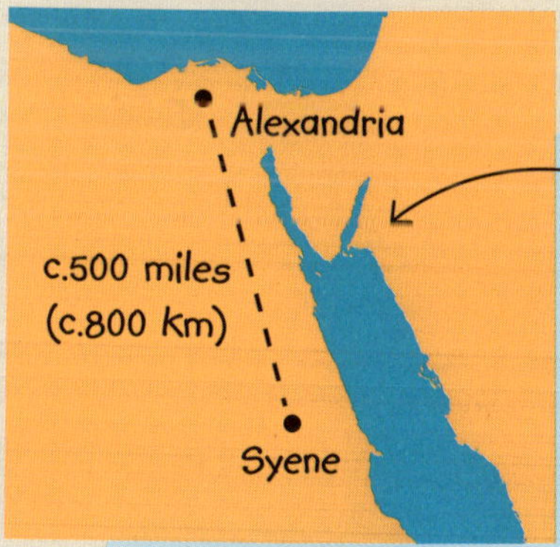

By counting steps, the Egyptians knew the distance from Alexandria to Syene was about 500 miles (800 km) in today's units.

4 In ancient Egypt, distances between places were measured by specialist walkers. Eratosthenes found out the distance between Syene and Alexandria and now had all he needed to work out Earth's circumference ...

Specialist walkers took regular strides to improve the accuracy of their measurements.

Doing the math

ANGLES AND SECTORS

With his measurements, Eratosthenes could work out the circumference of Earth using his knowledge of angles and circle sectors.

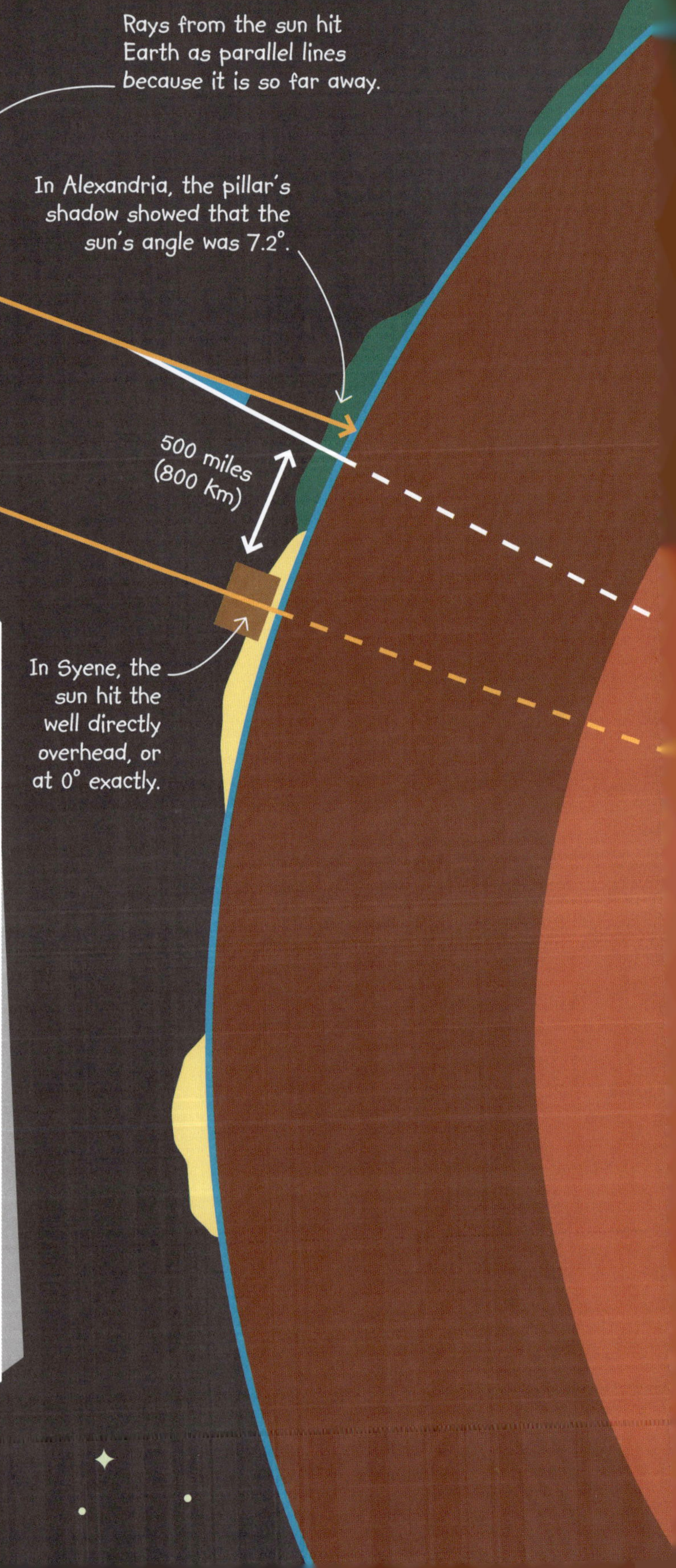

Angles

Eratosthenes knew that when a line cuts through a pair of parallel lines, the angles it forms with each line are identical. These are known as pairs of angles.

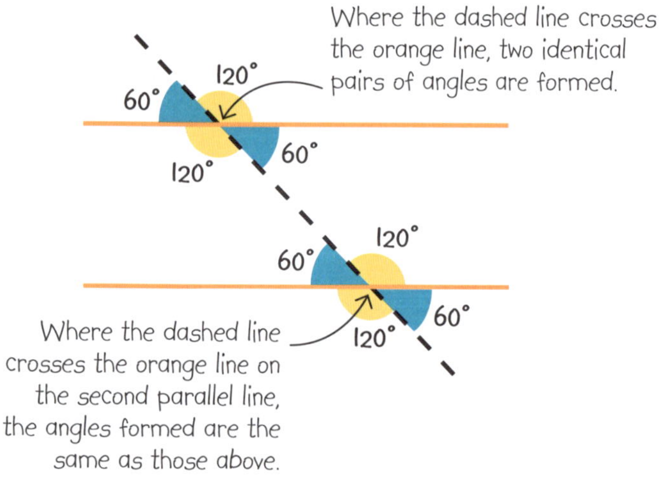

The angle of the light hitting the pillar in Alexandria was 7.2°. Eratosthenes imagined two lines, one passing through the pillar and the other passing through the well in Syene, eventually meeting in the center of Earth. These two imagined lines met at an angle of 7.2°, matching the angle of the sun's light as it hit the pillar.

Circle sectors

A sector is a portion of a circle formed when two straight lines that radiate out from the circle's center meet the part of the circumference between the two lines (called the arc). Imagine it as a pizza slice. You can work out the size of the sector (or pizza slice) by comparing its angle with the angle of a full circle (or the whole pizza).

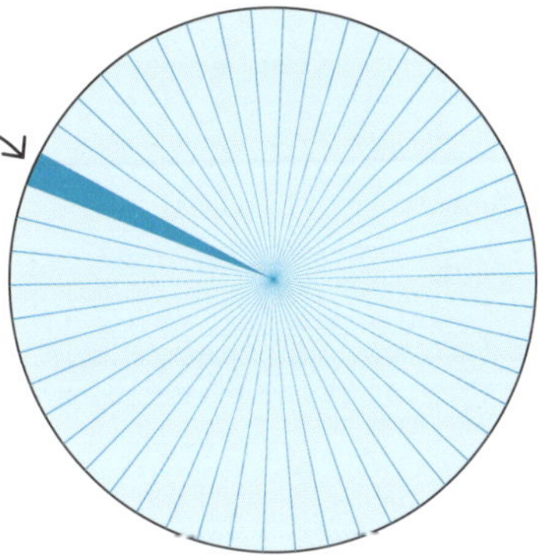

Together, the arc (the distance between the two cities at Earth's surface) and the two lines extending to Earth's center formed a circle sector.

The final calculation

Eratosthenes knew that Earth is a sphere, and so its circumference forms a circle (which has 360°). All he had to do to work out the circumference was calculate the distance between Alexandria and Syene as a proportion of a circle. To do this, he divided 360 by 7.2.

$$360 \div 7.2 = 50$$

This meant that the distance between the two cities was 1/50 of the entire world. So when he found out they were 500 miles (800 km) apart, he multiplied this number by 50.

$$500 \text{ miles} \times 50 = 25{,}000 \text{ miles}$$

Thanks to technology and mathematics, we now know the precise circumference of Earth is 24,901 miles (40,075 km), so Eratosthenes was remarkably close!

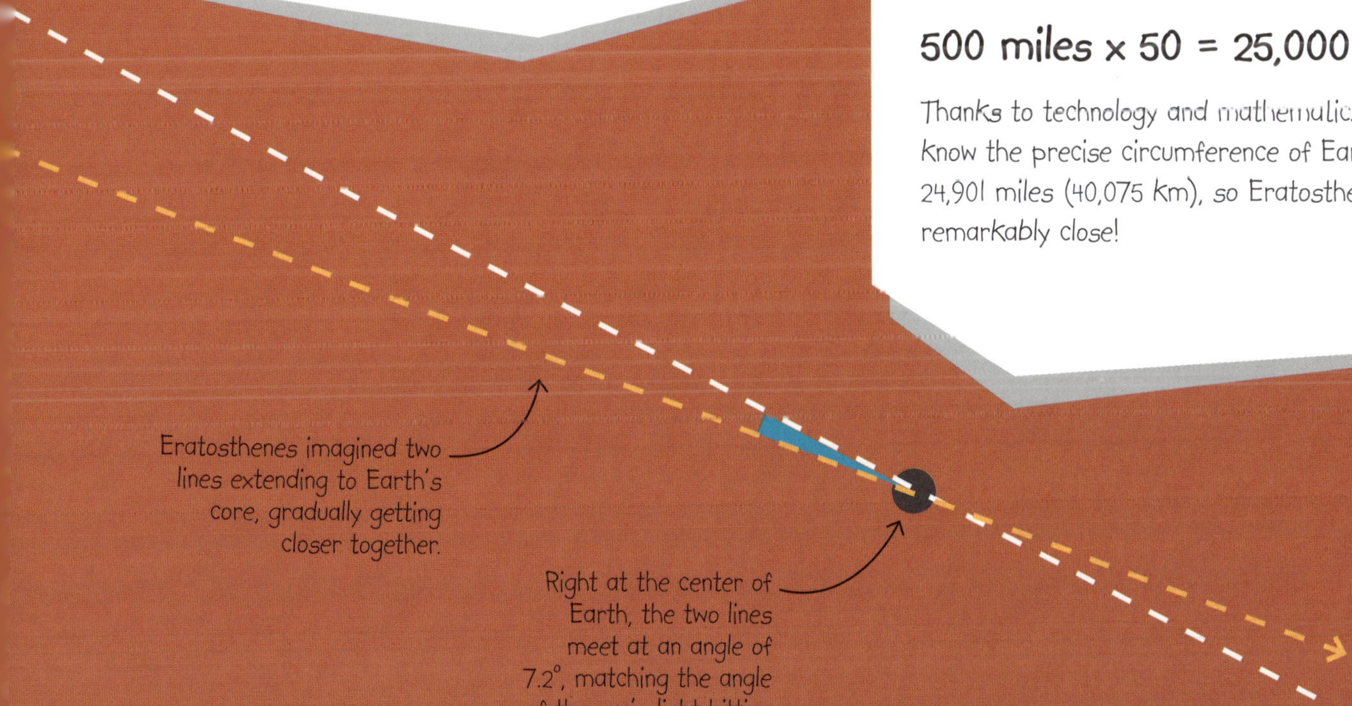

Eratosthenes imagined two lines extending to Earth's core, gradually getting closer together.

Right at the center of Earth, the two lines meet at an angle of 7.2°, matching the angle of the sun's light hitting the pillar in Alexandria.

CROSS-SECTION OF EARTH

HOW TO GET A PIECE OF PI

Take any circle, whether it's as small as a button or as large as the sun. Now divide the distance around it (the circumference) by the distance from one side to the other (the diameter), passing through the circle's center point. The answer is always 3.14159... This number goes on and on and on. We call this number "pi" and represent it with the symbol "π"—the first letter in the Greek word for circumference (*periphereia*). Pi is incredibly important in anything involving circles or curves.

WHAT IS PI?

The distance around the outside of a circle is called the circumference (c), and the distance across the middle is called the diameter (d). The value for pi never changes, because the relationship between the diameter and the circumference is always the same: when one increases, the other increases in proportion.

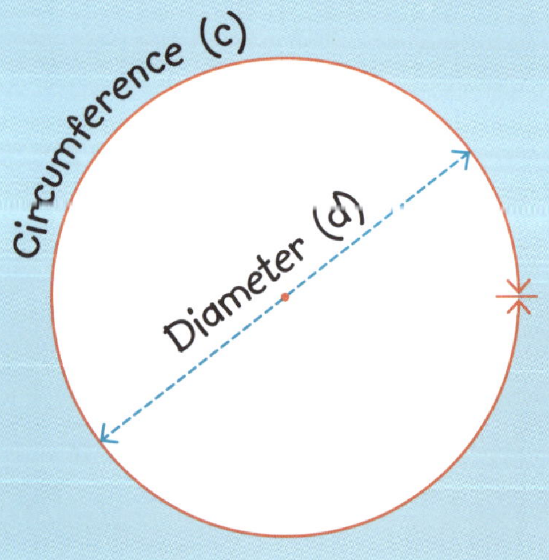

$$\frac{\text{Circumference}}{\text{Diameter}} = \pi = 3.14159...$$

DID YOU KNOW?

Space pi

Pi is incredibly useful for understanding outer space: from how planets move, to plotting spaceflights, to even calculating the size of the universe!

PI IN NATURE

English mathematician Alan Turing produced mathematical equations in 1952 that described how patterns in nature are formed. His work showed that pi has a role in patterns such as a leopard's spots, the placement of leaves on a plant, and the striped pattern of a zebra.

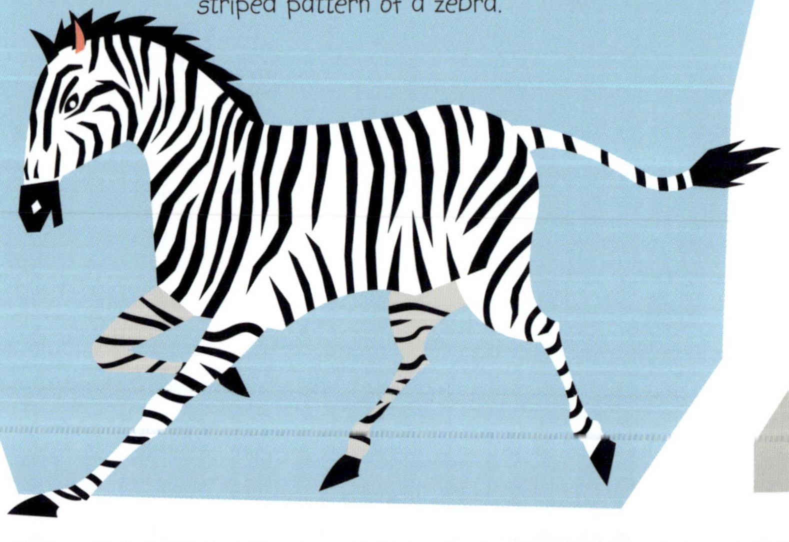

IRRATIONAL PI

Pi is an irrational number, which means it can't be written as a fraction. It goes on forever, without any repetition or pattern to the numbers. For this reason, it is often used to test a computer's processing power to demonstrate how fast and capable a computer is at handling tasks.

Currently we can calculate pi to 31,415,926,535,897 decimal places.

HOW TO TELL THE TIME

Imagine not knowing what time of day or year it is! You wouldn't know the best time to plant or harvest food, or even know how long it was before the day ended. We now know that Earth turns on its axis once every day—we divide the day into 24 hours—and that it completes an orbit of the sun in roughly 365 days and 6 hours, which we call a year.

LUNAR CALENDAR

The oldest-surviving calendar is a lunar calendar dug into the ground at Warren Field, Scotland. Experts think that hunter-gatherers used the 29-day lunar cycle to predict when migrating animals would return.

c. 8000 BCE

c. 1500 BCE

c. 1500 BCE

SUN SHADOWS

The ancient Egyptians and Babylonians were the first civilizations to use sundials, which track the movement of the sun. A stick or pillar—called a *gnomon*—casts a shadow, and the shadow's length and position are used to roughly indicate the hour.

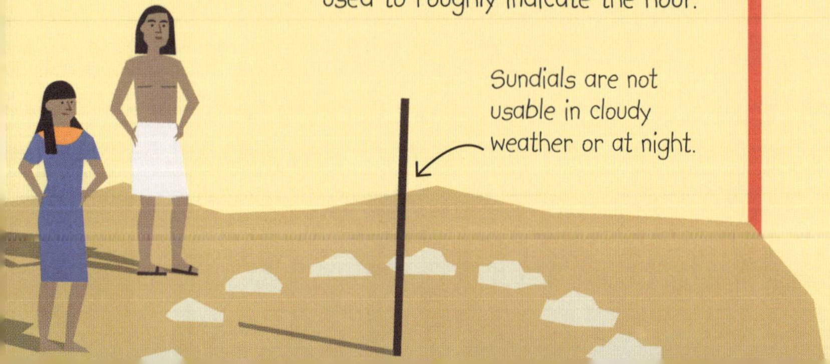

WATER AND FLAME

The Egyptians divided the day into two 12-hour periods and used the consistent movement of water, draining slowly from one large bowl into another, to track each period. Much later, candle clocks, popular in China and Japan, used a burning candle instead of moving water to mark time passing.

MAYA CALENDAR

The ancient Maya were fascinated by time and made some incredibly accurate calendars. The combined Maya calendar is actually three interlocking calendars: the 260-day religious calendar (*Tzolkin*), the 365-day solar calendar (*Haab*), and the 1,872,000-day Long Count, which counted down to the day the Maya believed the world would end and be reborn.

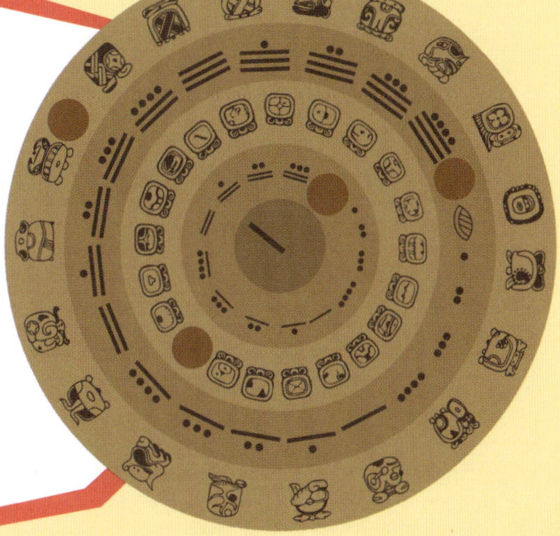

Every 52 years, the *Tzolkin* and *Haab* calendars would come back in sync with each other; this is called a "Calendar Round."

c. 500 BCE

THE ISLAMIC CALENDAR

Based on the Moon's cycle, the Islamic calendar has 12 months, each 29–30 days long. The first day of the Islamic year marks Hijra, when the Prophet Muhammad traveled from Mecca to Medina.

45 BCE

622 CE

c. 750

JULIAN CALENDAR

Roman dictator Julius Caesar reformed the out-of-sync Roman calendar to align with the seasons. His Julian calendar calculated a solar year to be 365 days and 6 hours. The year was split into 12 months. A 366-day "leap year" every fourth year accounted for the solar year's extra 6 hours.

After Caesar died, the seventh month was called "July" after him. The eighth month was named "August" after Caesar's heir, Augustus.

SANDS OF TIME

An hourglass reliably measures time by allowing a constant trickle of sand to pass through the thin neck between two glass bulbs. Thought originally to have been invented in the 8th century, the hourglass became popular on ships centuries later because, unlike water clocks, it didn't spill, freeze, or condense.

MECHANICAL MARVELS

It took a while for mechanical clocks that actually worked to appear. One of the earliest was made by Chinese inventor Zhang Sixun. Building on the work of earlier Chinese clockmakers, Zhang developed a mechanism called an "escapement" that rhythmically rotated back and forth to make his astronomical clock tower tick at a fixed pace.

PENDULUM CLOCKS

Dutch scientist Christiaan Huygens made the first clock with a pendulum (a rod that is fixed at one end and has a swinging weight on the other). It worked with the clock's escapement to reduce the inaccuracy of its timekeeping from 15 minutes per day to 15 seconds.

977

1582

1656

1761

GREGORIAN CALENDAR

Pope Gregory XIII corrected the Julian calendar, which was wrong by 11 minutes every year. This reform caused a jump of 10 days, so October 4, 1582, was followed by October 15, 1582! The Gregorian calendar, as it came to be known, was slow to be adopted but is the most widely used calendar in the world today.

LONGITUDE RESOLVED

The incredibly precise marine chronometer clock, made by English inventor John Harrison, kept time to within 3 seconds a day. It also cracked a long-standing problem for navigators, allowing them to work out their longitude (how far east or west they were) by using the difference in time from where they were to a reference time on land, provided by the chronometer.

REVOLUTION!

After a revolution against King Louis XVI, France revolutionized time. The country adopted a new calendar starting in September, with three 10-day weeks in a month. Clocks changed to a system of 10-hour days with 100 minutes per hour and 100 seconds per minute. The idea was completely abandoned in 1805.

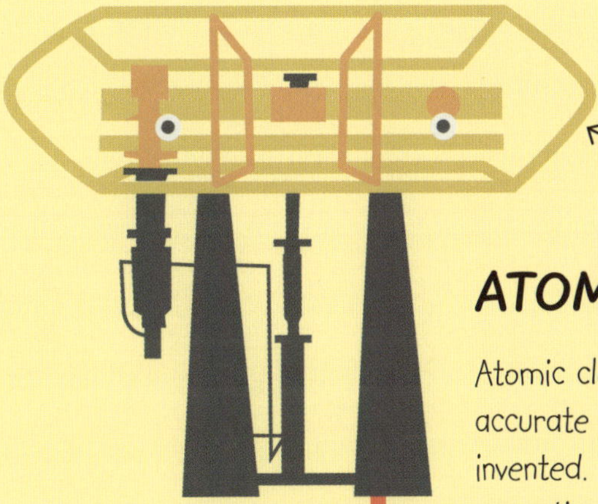

ATOMIC TIME

Atomic clocks keep the most accurate time of any timepiece invented. They use the rapidly repeating vibrations of atoms' electrons to keep time. Most use the element caesium.

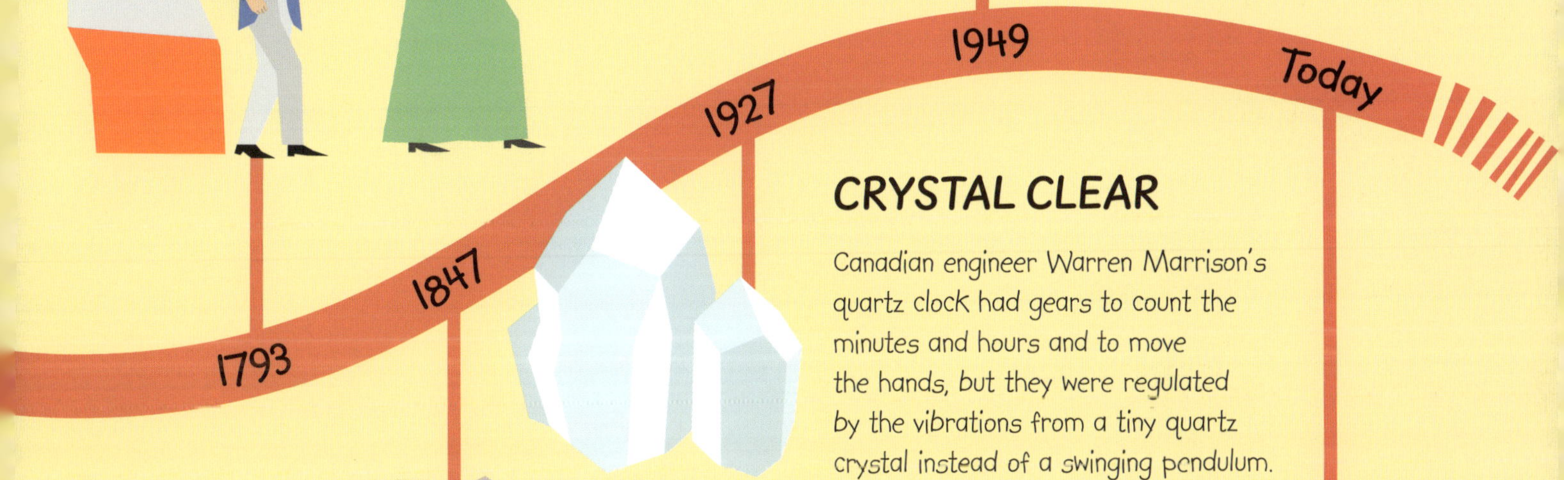

CRYSTAL CLEAR

Canadian engineer Warren Marrison's quartz clock had gears to count the minutes and hours and to move the hands, but they were regulated by the vibrations from a tiny quartz crystal instead of a swinging pendulum. Quartz clocks were more accurate than any other timekeeper, only gaining or losing 1 second in 3 years.

GREENWICH MEAN TIME

Before railways, each town kept its own time, shown on its town clock. As railways spread, a universally agreed time became necessary as travelers needed to know when to expect to depart and arrive. As a result, each country switched to a standard, unified time. In the UK, this happened in 1847, when Greenwich Mean Time (GMT) was adopted.

LEAP SECONDS

Every so often, "leap seconds" are added to the time to counteract irregularities in Earth's rotation. As most people use digital devices connected to the internet to tell the time, these updates are pushed out to billions of time-keeping devices in seconds with minimal fuss.

HOW TO USE COORDINATES

How would you describe the position of a fly buzzing around your bedroom? That was the question that bugged 17th-century French mathematician and philosopher René Descartes as he lay in bed one morning. As he considered the problem, he dreamed up coordinates, a brilliantly simple system that uses numbers to describe where something is. From a tiny fly on a ceiling, to huge ships at sea, and even planets within the solar system, coordinates can be used to describe the position of just about anything.

Doing the math
COORDINATES

Descartes' coordinates system uses two numbers to describe the position of an object based on its distance from the starting point of 0. The first coordinate is the horizontal position (how far to the left or right it is from the starting point) and the second one is the vertical position (how far above or below the starting point it is).

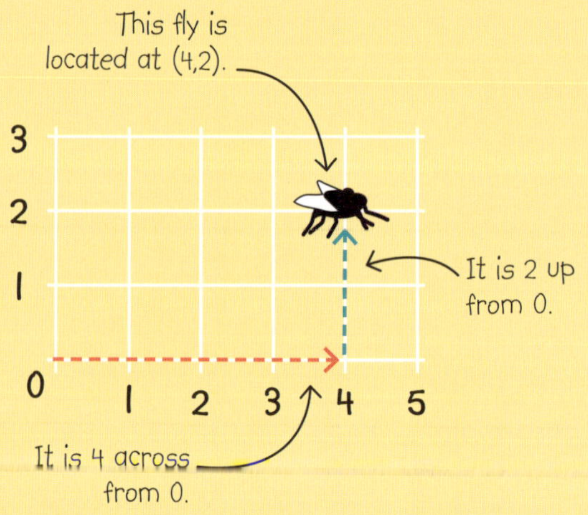

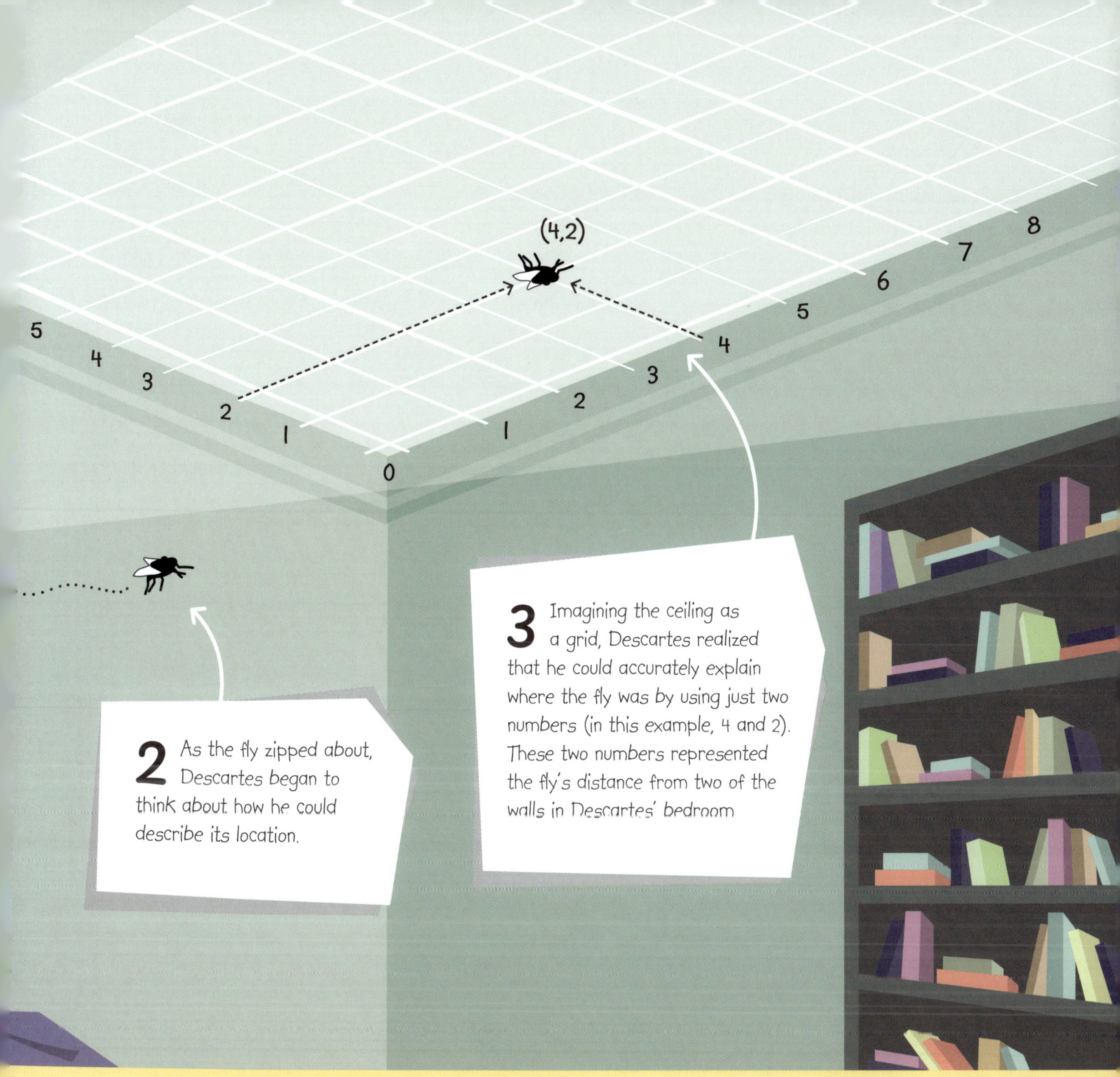

2 As the fly zipped about, Descartes began to think about how he could describe its location.

3 Imagining the ceiling as a grid, Descartes realized that he could accurately explain where the fly was by using just two numbers (in this example, 4 and 2). These two numbers represented the fly's distance from two of the walls in Descartes' bedroom

We can take Descartes' imaginary ceiling grid a step further and plot the fly's position on the ceiling using a graph. The fly is represented with a dot. On a graph, the horizontal line is known as the x-axis and the vertical line is called the y-axis. The number of the fly's horizontal position is known as the x-coordinate and the one for its vertical position is called the y-coordinate.

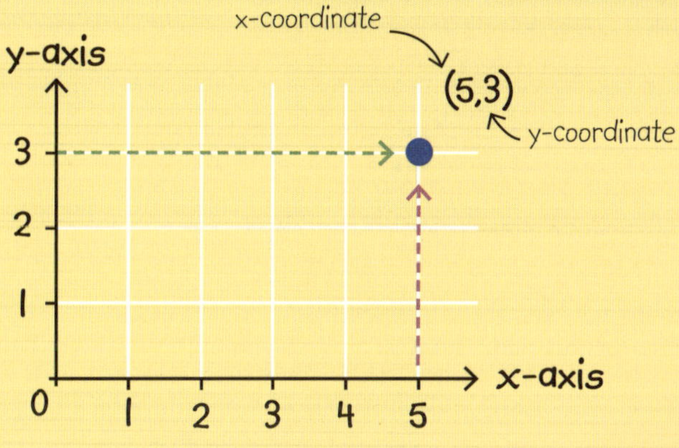

Graph showing position of fly

NEGATIVE COORDINATES

But what if you want to describe the position of something that is behind or below the starting point of 0? To do this, you can extend the x- and y-axes so that they include negative numbers, too. On the x-axis, the negative numbers appear to the left of 0 and on the y-axis, they are below 0.

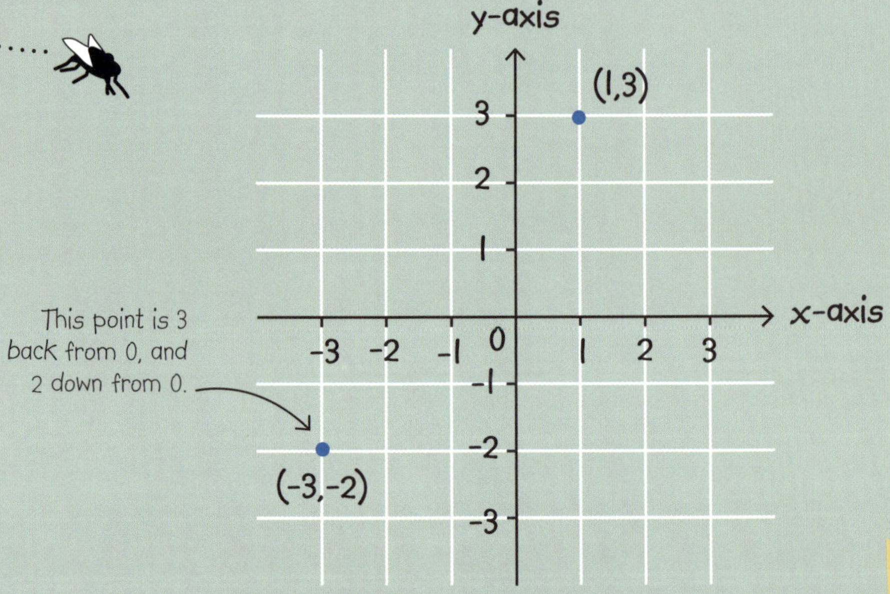

TWO AND THREE DIMENSIONS

A graph with just x- and y-axes works in two dimensions. But mathematicians sometimes add a third dimension on a new line known as the z-axis. This line also meets the x- and y-axes at point 0. The z-axis lets mathematicians plot the location of a three-dimensional object in a three-dimensional space, such as a box in a room.

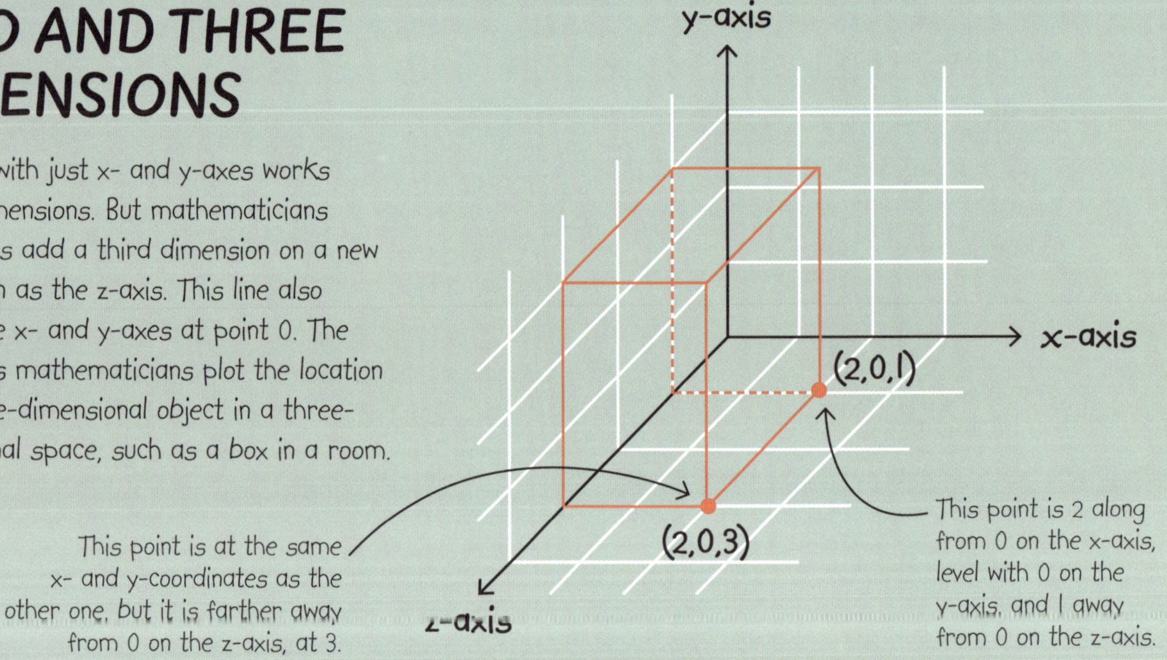

REAL WORLD

Archaeological digs

When archaeologists carry out a dig, they use tape to mark out a grid over the site. They then use coordinates taken from the grid to record exactly where they found different historical objects during their search.

TRY IT OUT

HOW TO FIND LOST TREASURE

You've found an old map of a treasure island with a mysterious riddle on the back. Follow the riddle's instructions to draw a route on the map and crack the location of the treasure.

Climb northwest from Monkey Beach,
And Snowy Mountain you will reach.
Continue north to Dead Man's Cave,
Then head southeast to Pirate's Grave.
Hike southwest to cross your route,
X marks the spot of the buried loot.

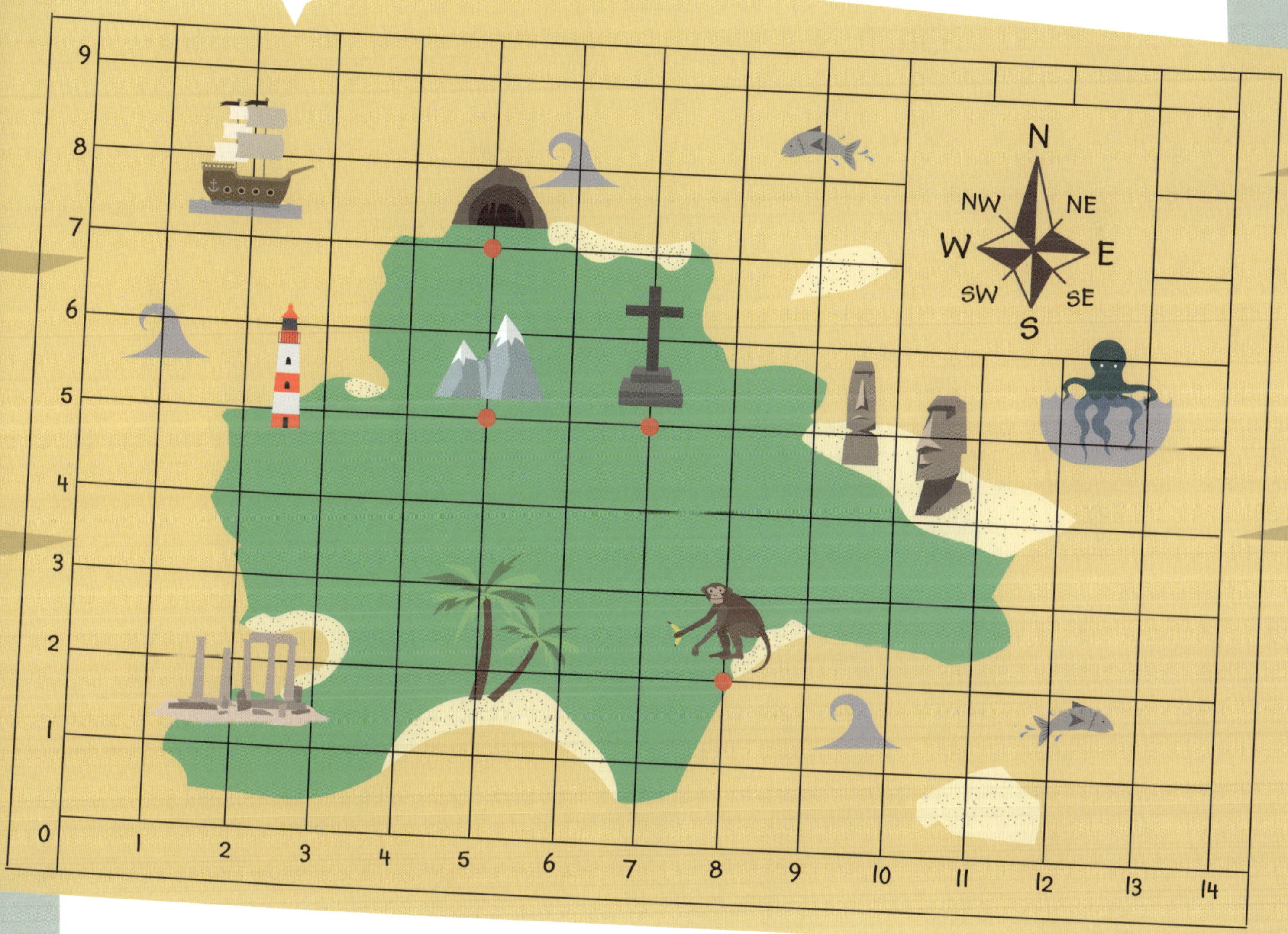

Now try making your own treasure map. Show your friends how coordinates work and see if they can locate the treasure. You could even create a map of your house and hide some treasure for your friends to find!

WHAT'S THE POINT OF

PATTERNS AND SEQUENCES?

Patterns and sequences are everywhere in math, from a sequence as simple as the two-times table to the mystery of prime numbers. Throughout history, we've used patterns and sequences to keep our secrets safe with uncrackable codes and ciphers. And today, investigating patterns and sequences can teach us about nature, too – they even help to explain the eruptions of a geyser.

HOW TO PREDICT A COMET

In 17th-century England, mathematician Edmond Halley was studying some old records of astronomical observations. As he made a list of comet sightings over the years, he realized that one comet might actually be coming back over and over again. Halley predicted the comet's return in 1758 and, when 1758 came around, was proved right. Halley didn't live to see his prediction come true, but the comet was named after him, sealing his place in history.

1 Astronomers in 1531, 1607, and 1682 had reported seeing a comet in the night sky.

2 Halley recognized a pattern and realized that the same comet was coming back about every 76 years.

Doing the math
ARITHMETIC SEQUENCES

In spotting the predictable pattern of the comet's orbit, Halley recognized a mathematical sequence. A pattern in which the numbers increase (or decrease) by a fixed amount each time is called an arithmetic sequence. The amount by which the number changes is called the common difference.

28 47 66 ...

+19 +19 +19

Common difference

DID YOU KNOW?

Orbiting comets

Comets are chunks of ice, rock, and dust that orbit (travel around) the sun in elliptical (oval-shaped) paths. Comets that get close to the sun, like Halley's Comet, often develop long "tails" of gas that glow in the night sky.

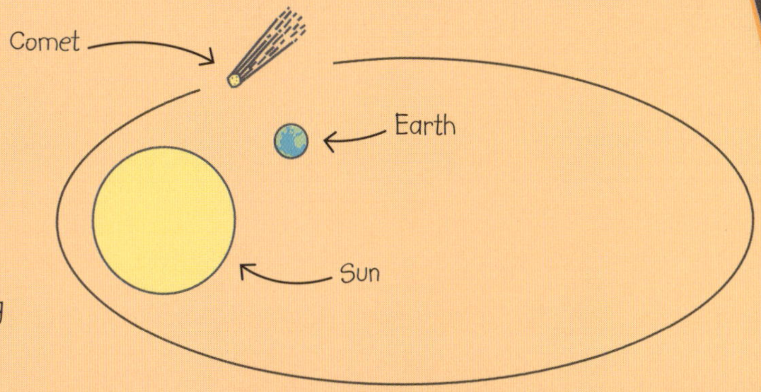

3 Halley predicted that the comet would return in 1758. He was proved correct, and the comet has returned every 76 years or so since.

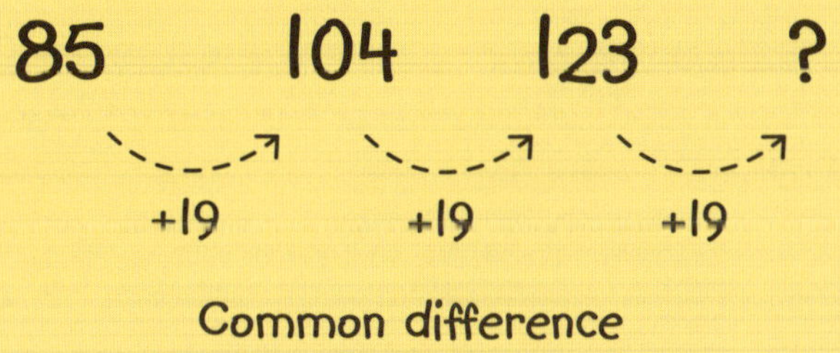

The common difference in this arithmetic sequence is 19. To find the next number, you just need to add on the common difference again. Halley's Comet isn't a perfect sequence—it returns on average every 76 years but can appear a year or two earlier or later because of the gravitational pull of the outer planets (and Halley was clever enough to realize this too).

HOW ARITHMETIC SEQUENCES WORK

Here's a simple arithmetic sequence with a common difference of 3. To find the next number, you just need to add 3.

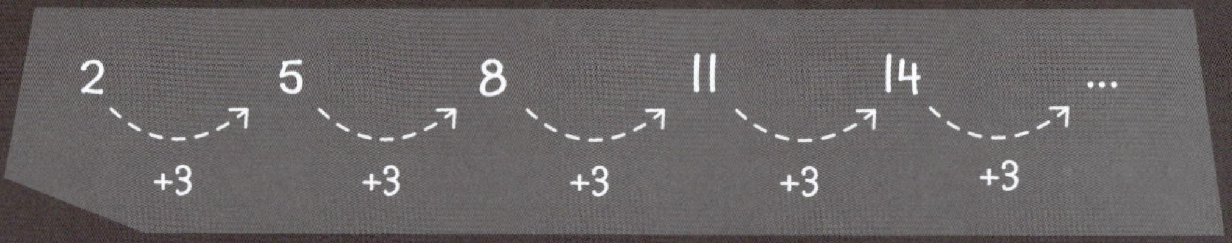

We can also describe any arithmetic sequence, including this one, with letters:

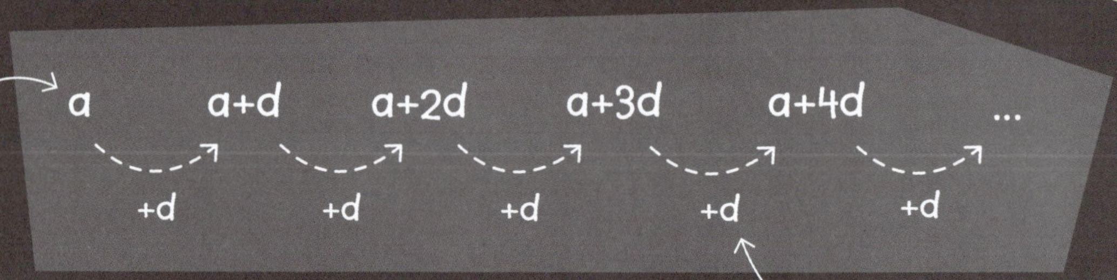

When writing in this way, a is the first number (in this case, 2) and d is the common difference (in this case, 3). The next term will be a + 5d, so by translating the letters into numbers, we can work it out as 2 + (5 x 3) = 17.

FOLDING NUMBERS

In the 1780s, a German schoolteacher gave his class of 8-year-olds a problem to keep them busy for a while. He asked them to add up all the numbers from 1 to 100:

1 + 2 + 3 + ... + 98 + 99 + 100 = ?

To his surprise, one student came up with the answer in just 2 minutes. They had no calculators back then, so how did he do it?

The boy "folded" the numbers so that 1 joins with 100, 2 joins with 99, and so on. Each pair of numbers now added up to 101. Since there were 50 pairs of numbers, all the boy now had to do was multiply 50 by 101, which gave him the answer 5,050.

FINDING THE NTH NUMBER

But what if we want to find the 21st number in a sequence? Or the 121st? Writing out 21 numbers would take too long, so you need to create a formula.

We can find the answer by using the nth number formula, where n is the position of the number in the sequence you want to find out.

a represents the first number in the sequence.

d represents the common difference.

$$a+(n-1)d$$

n represents the position in the sequence you want to find.

n – 1 is the number of times you multiply the common difference (d) by. Because d is added to every number in the sequence except the first, we subtract 1 × d (in other words one amount of d).

We multiply n-1 (in this case, 21 - 1 = 20) by the common difference (in this case, 3), then add this to a (in this case, 2).

$$2+(21-1)\times 3 = 62$$

So the 21st number in the sequence starting 2, 5, 8 ... will be 62.

TRY IT OUT

HOW TO COUNT SEATS

A school theater has 15 rows, with 12 seats in the front row near the narrow stage. The theater widens as it stretches back, and the number of seats in each row increases by 2.

Using the formula for finding the nth number, can you work out how many seats there are in the back row?

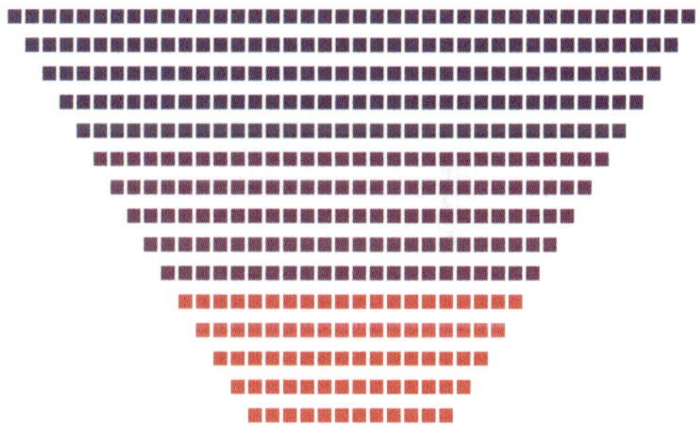

100 is added to 1, 99 is added to 2, 98 is added to 3, and so on.

$$1 + 2 + 3 + ... + 98 + 99 + 100$$

101

101

101

Each of these pairs adds up to 101.

The boy's name was Carl Friedrich Gauss, and he would go on to become one of the world's greatest mathematicians.

REAL WORLD

Repeating geyser

The famous Old Faithful geyser in Yellowstone National Park is so named because it erupts every 90 minutes or so. But the pattern isn't an exact arithmetic sequence as the gaps between eruptions vary from one to two hours.

HOW TO BECOME A TRILLIONAIRE

What comes next: 1, 2, 4, 8, 16 ...? The answer is 32. Each new number in this ordered list of numbers, or "sequence," is found by multiplying the previous number by 2. What seem like small increases in the sequence at first soon start to become enormous, as this Indian legend about a king's defeat during a game of chess shows ....

1 After losing a game of chess to a wise traveler, the king offered a reward to the victor, who modestly requested some rice for each square of the chessboard. He asked for one grain of rice for the first square, two for the next, and so on, doubling every time.

2 At first, this sounded reasonable enough to the king. However, as the numbers continued to double, the piles of rice he owed the victor started to become enormous.

Doing the math
GEOMETRIC SEQUENCES

The amount of rice on each square of the chessboard is found by multiplying the amount on the previous square by a fixed amount (in this case, 2), known as the common ratio. A sequence that increases by multiplying each number by a common ratio is known as a geometric sequence.

Multiplying grains of rice

3 The King eventually owed his opponent 18 million trillion grains of rice—enough to bury his entire Kingdom in rice!

DID YOU KNOW?

Folding paper

If you fold an imaginary piece of paper in half and repeat the process 54 times, it will eventually be thick enough to reach the Sun. It's impossible to fold a real piece of paper that many times though—because it will become too thick to bend!

1 → ×2 → 2 → ×2 → 4 → ×2 → 8 → ×2 → 16

Multiplying numbers

If you swap the rice for numbers, you can see how the sequence works. It only takes four steps to get from 1 to 16, and another four steps would take you all the way to 256! You can see how the victor's piles of rice became so huge so quickly.

THE ROYAL CHESSBOARD

Here, the number of rice grains on each chessboard square are written out in figures. Now you can see just how quickly the numbers increase!

Can you say the number in the bottom right square of the chessboard out loud?

REAL WORLD

Carbon-14 dating

Scientists use geometric sequences to figure out how long ago plants and animals lived. With each 5,730 years that passes, the quantity of a substance called carbon-14 left in an organism's remains falls by half. By knowing how much carbon-14 was in the organism when it died, scientists can tell when it lived by how much is left in its remains now.

1	2	4	8	16	32	64	128
256	512	1,024	2,048	4,096	8,192	16,384	32,768
65,536	131,072	262,144	524,288	1,048, 576	2,097, 152	4,194, 304	8,388, 608
16,777, 216	33,554, 432	67,108, 864	134,217, 728	268,435, 456	536,870, 912	1,073, 741,824	2,147, 483,648
4,294, 967,296	8,589, 934,592	17,179, 869,184	34,359, 738,368	68,719, 476,736	137,438, 953,472	274,877, 906,944	549,755, 813,888
1,099,511, 627,776	2,199,023, 255,552	4,398,046, 511,104	8,796, 093,022, 208	17,592, 186,044, 416	35,184, 372,088, 832	70,368, 744,177, 664	140,737, 488,355, 328
281,474, 976,710, 656	562,949, 953,421, 312	1,125, 899,906, 842,624	2,251, 799,813, 685,248	4,503, 599,627, 370,496	9,007, 199,254, 740,992	18,014, 398,509, 481,984	36,028, 797,018, 963,968
72,057, 594,037, 927,936	144,115, 188,075, 855,872	288,230, 376,151, 711,744	576,460, 752,303, 423,488	1,152,921, 504,606, 846,976	2,305,843, 009,213, 693,952	4,611,686, 018,427, 387,904	9,223,372, 036,854, 775,808

POWERS

Powers tell you how many times to multiply a number by itself. You can show how the rice increases each time using powers. They are written as small numbers at the top right of the number you want to multiply by itself. So 2^2 is the same as saying 2×2, and 4^3 is the same as $4 \times 4 \times 4$.

This is the number at the start of the sequence.

n means the position of the number in the sequence.

$$1 \times 2^{(n-1)}$$

The common ratio in this sequence is 2.

You have to subtract 1 from n, because the first number in the sequence isn't multiplied by the common ratio.

Use n-1 to find the 6th number in the sequence, which is 6-1 or 5.

$$1 \times 2^{(6-1)} = 1 \times 2^5 = 32$$

The 6th number in the sequence is 32.

You can find out the number for any position in the King's chessboard sequence using this formula. You need to know three things—the number at the start of the sequence (in this case, 1), the common ratio (the number it's being multiplied by—in this case, 2), and the position of the number in the sequence minus 1.

Can you find out what the 20th number in the sequence is? You might need a calculator!

TRY IT OUT

HOW TO BOOST YOUR SAVINGS

You have two coins. You save them in a bank with a very generous interest rate. By year 2, you have six coins. How many will you have by year 5?

The number of coins follows a growth pattern from one year to the next. To figure out each year's coin total, the previous total is multiplied by three.

So by year 5, the total will be $2 \times 3^4 = 162$ coins.

Using the formula $2 \times 3^{n-1}$, can you work out how much money you'd have saved by year 15?

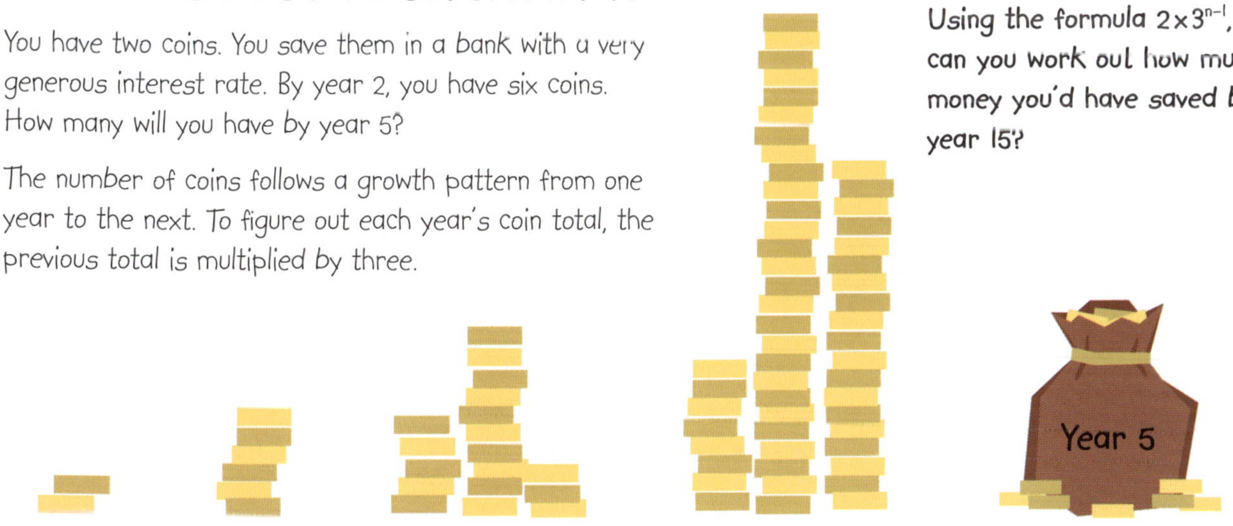

Year 1	Year 2	Year 3	Year 4	Year 5
2	$2 \times 3^1 = 6$	$2 \times 3^2 = 18$	$2 \times 3^3 = 54$	$2 \times 3^4 = 162$

HOW TO USE PRIME NUMBERS

A prime number is any whole number larger than 1 that you can't divide by whole numbers, other than itself and 1. For mathematicians, primes are the building blocks of math, because every number is either a prime or can be reached by multiplying primes together (which we call a "composite number").

PUZZLING PRIMES

A huge reason for mathematicians being interested in primes is that we know there are an infinite number of them yet we have not found a regular pattern to them. Also, 2 is the only even prime—the rest are all odd numbers.

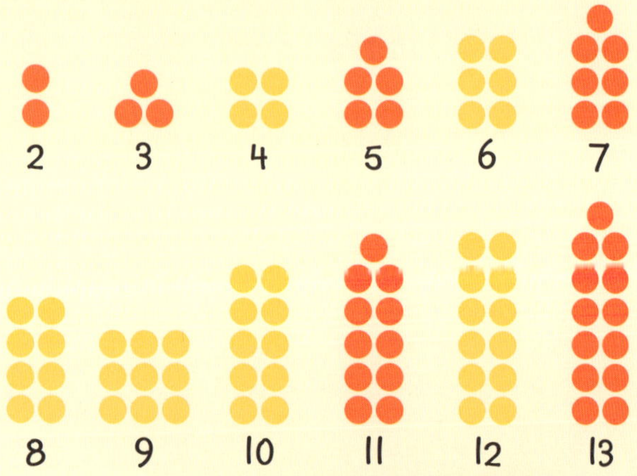

DID YOU KNOW?

Big primes

As of January 2019, the largest known prime is a number so big that it has 24,862,048 digits when written out.

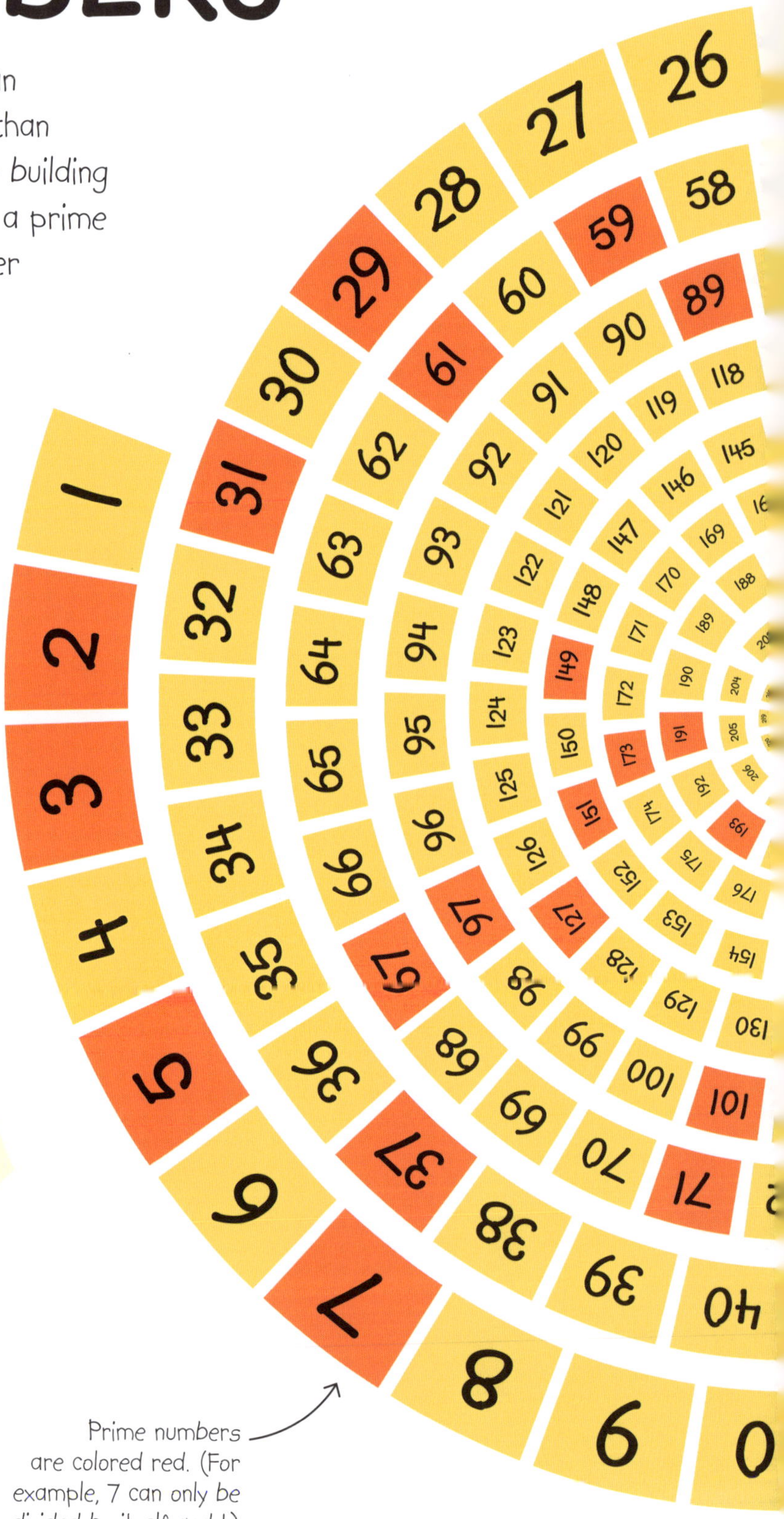

Prime numbers are colored red. (For example, 7 can only be divided by itself and 1.)

ONLINE SECURITY

When paying for things online, prime numbers are used to make an unbreakable secret code. The "lock" for the transaction is a huge number, and the "keys" are two prime factors (prime factors are prime numbers that you multiply together to get a composite number) that would take thousands of years to work out if you didn't know them, making the transaction secure.

PUZZLE

Try to break 589 into its two prime factors. (Use the prime wheel on the left!)

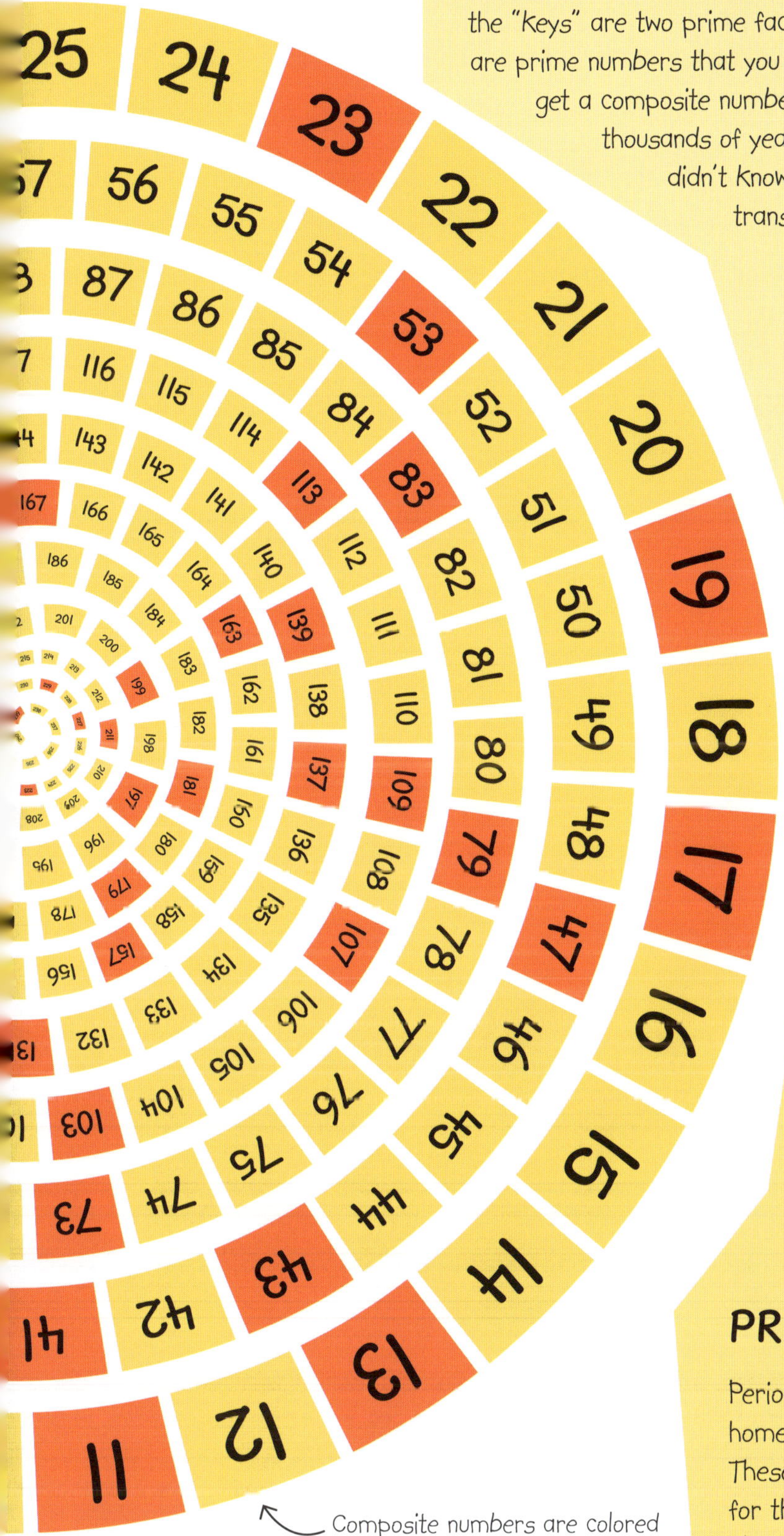

Composite numbers are colored yellow. (For example, 12 can be reached by multiplying the prime numbers 2 x 2 x 3.)

PRIME TIME

Periodical cicadas emerge from their underground homes every 13 or 17 years to breed and lay eggs. These prime-numbered schedules make it harder for their predators to rely on them for food and also make it easier for them to organize mating.

HOW TO GO ON FOREVER

Some things simply never end. Things that end are known as "finite" and things that don't are called "infinite." Infinity is not a number; it is more of an idea—a mind-bending concept that's almost impossible to imagine. It's endless and boundless and has led to some brain-twisting ideas in the world of math.

HILBERT'S HOTEL

German mathematician David Hilbert's thought experiment about a hotel with infinite rooms reveals the bizarre math of infinity:

1 The infinite hotel is full, but one day, a new guest arrives.

2 Because the hotel is infinite, there are always more rooms, so the owner asks all residents to move one room up, from room 1 to 2, room 2 to 3, and so on, so the new guest can have room 1. Therefore, Infinity + 1 = Infinity.

3 Shortly afterward, an infinite coach arrives with infinite guests. To make rooms available, the owner asks all guests to double their room number and move to the new number.

4 The residents are now in rooms with even numbers, so the infinite number of odd-numbered rooms are now available for the infinite number of new guests! This shows that 2 × Infinity = Infinity.

ZENO'S RACE

The ancient Greek mathematician Zeno used a story of a race between the legendary Greek hero Achilles and a tortoise to explain an idea about infinity. The tortoise gets a head start, but Achilles soon races to where the tortoise was. However, the tortoise has moved on a bit. Every time Achilles closes the distance, the tortoise extends it a fraction more. Zeno's silly story demonstrates why we have to be careful when working with the idea of infinity.

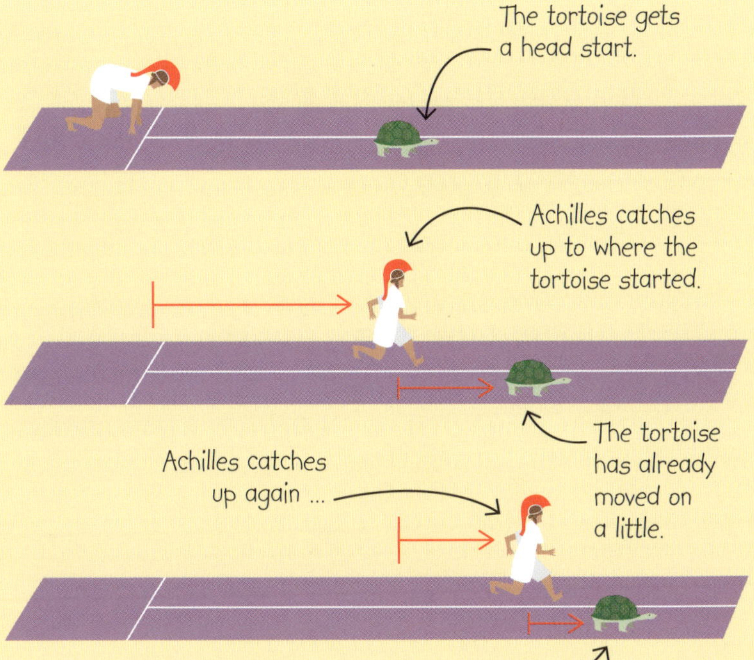

DID YOU KNOW?

Strange names

Large numbers are often given exotic names. A 1 with 100 zeros behind it is called a "googol," and a "googolplex" is a 1 with a googol of zeros behind it!

These numbers are written in powers (such as 10^7) to make them easier to write.

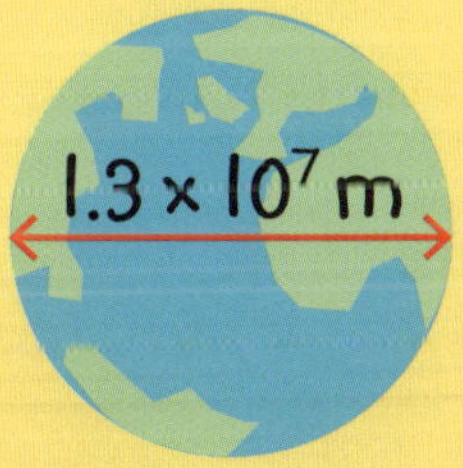

Diameter of Earth

Powers can be used to talk about incredibly small things by using a minus sign for the power (such as 10^{-10}).

Size of an atom

LARGE NUMBERS

Between the numbers we use in everyday life and infinity is a group of numbers that we call "large numbers." These numbers allow us to talk about things like the size of the observable universe (8.8×10^{26} m), the number of cells in the human body (estimated at 3.72×10^{13}), or the number of atoms in a substance.

HOW TO KEEP SECRETS

What's the best way to keep your secrets safe? Math! Throughout history, people have used codes (where whole words are replaced by letters, numbers, or symbols) and ciphers (where individual letters are substituted) to prevent their secrets from falling into the wrong hands.

DID YOU KNOW?

Cryptography

The word cryptography comes from the Greek word *cryptos*, meaning "hidden" or "secret," and "graphy" from the word *graphein*, meaning "to write."

FIRELIGHT MESSAGES

Ancient Greek soldiers used varying numbers of torches attached to walls to communicate information across battle positions. The number of lit torches corresponded to a particular row and column on a grid of letters (known as the "Polybius Square"). To spell "H," they lit two torches on the right (for row 2) and three torches on the left (for column 3).

	1	2	3	4	5
1	A	B	C	D	E
2	F	G	H	I	J
3	K	L	M	N	O
4	P	Q	R	S	T
5	U	V	W	X	Y/Z

2/3 1/5 3/2 3/2 3/5

= H E L L O

3rd century BCE

THE CAESAR SHIFT

To send secret instructions to his soldiers, Roman general Julius Caesar used a substitution cipher, now known as the "Caesar Shift." He converted each letter of the alphabet into a number, then added or subtracted a value that he had prearranged with his soldiers. If they'd agreed to add 3 to each letter, "a" became "d," "b" became "e," and so on.

a	b	c	d	e	f	g	h	i	j	k	l	m	n	o	p	q	r	s	t	u	v	w	x	y	z
D	E	F	G	H	I	J	K	L	M	N	O	P	Q	R	S	T	U	V	W	X	Y	Z	A	B	C

The top row is "plain text"—the original message before it is encrypted.

The bottom row is ciphered text—the message after it is encrypted.

PRYH DW GDZQ = move at dawn

PUZZLE

Crack a secret code

You've just stumbled on a top-secret message—but it's written in the Caesar Shift cipher. Can you work out what it says?

Message: ZH DUH QRW DORQH

c.50 BCE

9th century

POPULAR LETTERS

Arabic philosopher Al Kindi analyzed ciphers written in ancient texts. He realized that some letters were used more frequently than others. He deduced that, whatever language a coded message was written in, the most frequent symbol that appeared was probably the most popular letter in that particular language.

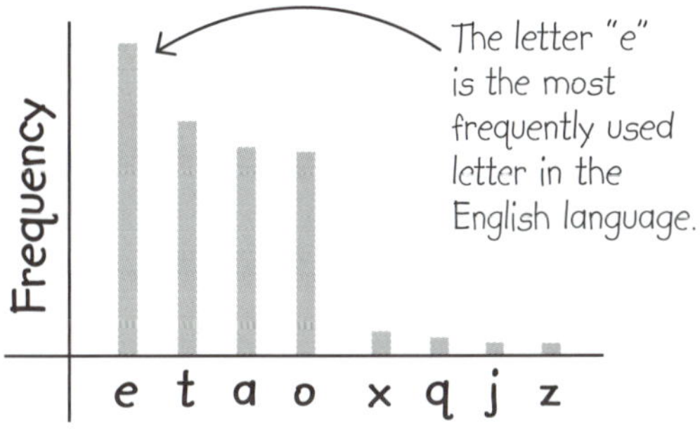

ROTATING DISKS

Italian architect Leon Battista Alberti created a device known as a cipher wheel. Two disks—one smaller, one bigger—were attached together at their centers with a pin. Both disks had different symbols and letters etched around their edges. To decipher a message—for example, F&MS&*F—the smaller wheel was rotated until the first letter of the coded message (in this case, "F") lined up with a prearranged starter letter (in this case, "s"). The remaining letters could then be worked out with the wheels in this position to give the original message: secrets. The Alberti Cipher was harder to crack than the Caesar Shift because encrypted messages also contained instructions to reset the position of the wheels every few letters.

HIDDEN IN BOOKS

Seventy years after the invention of the printing press made books widely available, Jacobus Silvestri developed the book cipher. This encryption uses a particular book prearranged by the sender and recipient. The words in the original message are located in the book, then given a number relating to their position on the page. The recipient must then use the numbers to locate the right words in the book.

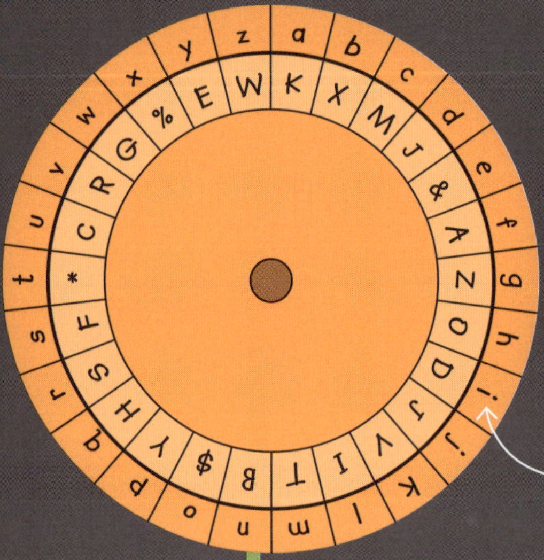

The inner circle of letters is the code. The outer circle of letters represents the original message.

1467

1526

1586

THE VIGENÈRE CIPHER

French cryptographer Blaise de Vigenère extended the Caesar Shift. He created a grid of multiple alphabets with which to encode each letter in a message. His almost impossible-to-break cipher remained uncracked for centuries.

MORSE CODE

For centuries, messengers had delivered secret information by foot or by horse. But the invention of the telegraph made it possible to communicate over long distances almost instantly. US inventor Samuel Morse came up with a system of dots (short electrical signals) and dashes (long electrical signals), which were tapped into the machine to represent letters of the alphabet.

International Morse Code

A	•—	N	—•
B	—•••	O	———
C	—•—•	P	•——•
D	—••	Q	——•—
E	•	R	•—•
F	••—•	S	•••
G	——•	T	—
H	••••	U	••—
I	••	V	•••—
J	•———	W	•——
K	—•—	X	—••—
L	•—••	Y	—•——
M	——	Z	——••

1586

1830s

PUZZLE

Send a secret message

Try writing a secret message to a friend using Morse Code.

UNCOVERING THE PLOT

Mary Stuart believed she was the rightful queen of England. She and her supporters plotted to assassinate Queen Elizabeth I, and they used a substitution cipher to communicate their plans. But Queen Elizabeth I's spymaster Sir Francis Walsingham intercepted a message and cracked their code, deciphering their treacherous plan. Mary Stuart was later executed for treason.

THE PIGPEN CIPHER

Pigpen was a type of substitution cipher used by imprisoned Union soldiers during the Civil War (1861–1865). The letters of the English alphabet had a set place in one of four different grids. The symbol used to represent each letter is made up of the shape of its particular grid. For letters J to R and W to Z, a dot is added to the shape.

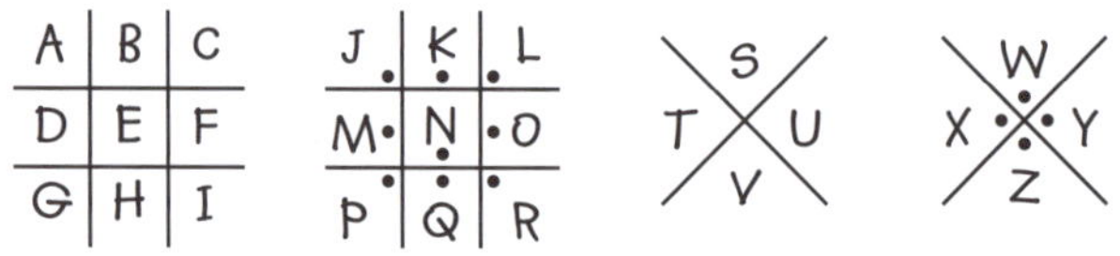

 = **escape this way**

1861–1865

1939–1945

WARTIME SECRETS

During World War II, the German military used a device known as the Enigma machine to encrypt information. The machine's almost uncrackable settings offered 158,000,000,000,000,000,000 possible solutions for every piece of coded text. A team of brilliant minds finally solved it, thanks to flaws in the Enigma machine discovered by mathematician Alan Turing. This allowed British cryptographers, who were mostly women, to read many of Germany's top-secret messages.

Mathematicians at Bletchley Park used a computing machine known as the "Bombe" to help them decipher secret German messages.

DID YOU KNOW?

The Enigma machine

The German military changed the settings on the Enigma machine daily, so the Allied code breakers were in a race against time to decipher their secret messages.

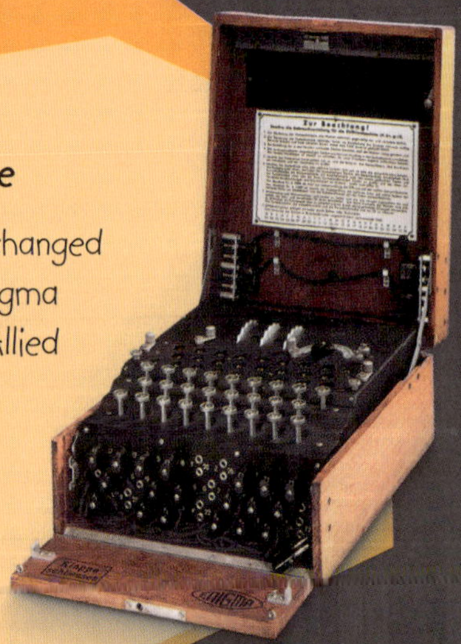

DID YOU KNOW?

Unsolved mystery

US artist Jim Sanborn's sculpture Kryptos (meaning "hidden"), outside the headquarters of the US Central Intelligence Agency (CIA), has a code built into its design. Since it was unveiled in 1990, neither amateur code breakers nor CIA cryptography experts have been able to crack it completely!

DIGITAL SECRETS

Today, ciphers help keep us safe online. Code makers are constantly working to create more and more complex codes to keep people's personal information safe against code breakers trying to access it.

1974

Today

MESSAGING ALIENS

Scientists broadcast a radio message from the Arecibo Observatory in Puerto Rico toward star cluster M13 at the edge of our galaxy in the hope that it might be intercepted and read by aliens. It will take almost 25,000 years for the message to reach the star cluster and the same amount of time for a reply to come back. The message was written in binary code (a system that uses 1s and 0s to represent letters). It usually appears in black and white.

When displayed as a picture, the Arecibo message looks like this.

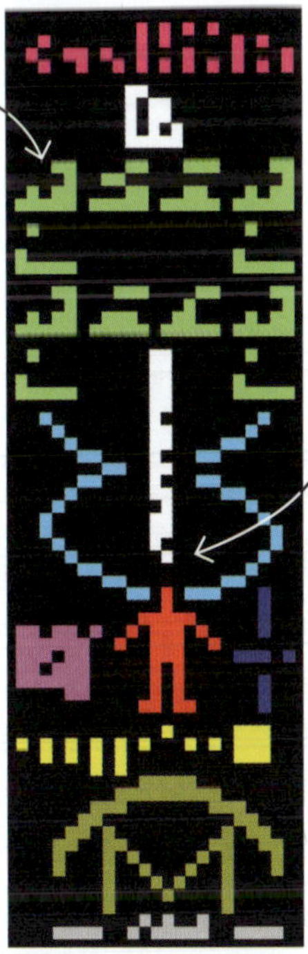

The message includes information about human DNA and a map of the solar system showing Earth's location.

WHAT'S THE POINT OF

DATA AND STATISTICS?

We live in an information age and are surrounded by more data and statistics than ever before in history. Mathematicians have developed lots of ways of collecting, understanding, and visualizing this information to help us make sense of it all. Math is full of quick tips to estimate rough quantities and formulas to analyze data in precise detail, allowing us to find out more about ourselves and the world around us.

HOW TO IMPRESS WITH A GUESS

It's not always possible to do exact math calculations on the spot, so mathematicians often make estimates instead. Estimation can give you a reasonable idea of what the approximate answer to a question is. When faced with a seemingly impossible calculation, an ancient Indian royal realized that he could use his estimation skills to make a very good guess.

1 According to an old Indian legend, King Rituparna, a brilliant mathematician, once boasted to his companion that he knew how many leaves there were on a particular tree.

2 Unconvinced, his companion cut down the tree and counted all the leaves by hand. The King was almost exactly right! But how did he do it?

Doing the math

ROUNDING AND ESTIMATING

King Rituparna hadn't actually counted each leaf on the tree. Instead, he estimated. To do this, he first counted the number of leaves on just a few twigs. Of the ones he counted, most twigs had roughly 20 leaves.

19 leaves 20 leaves 21 leaves

The King then needed to know how many twigs there were on each branch. The branches he counted had between 4 and 6 twigs, so he guessed that most branches had about 5 twigs each.

4 twigs 6 twigs 5 twigs

20 leaves x 5 twigs
x 10 branches
= 1000 leaves

Finally, the King counted the number of branches—this was a smaller number, so he could count them exactly instead of estimating. He counted 10 branches, then multiplied all the numbers together to find that the tree had around 1,000 leaves.

ROUNDING

Rounding means changing a number to a value that is close to it, which often makes calculations easier. Imagine something was between 18 and 19 cm in length. If you measured it exactly, it might be 18.7 cm, which you could round up to 19 cm to make your calculations simpler.

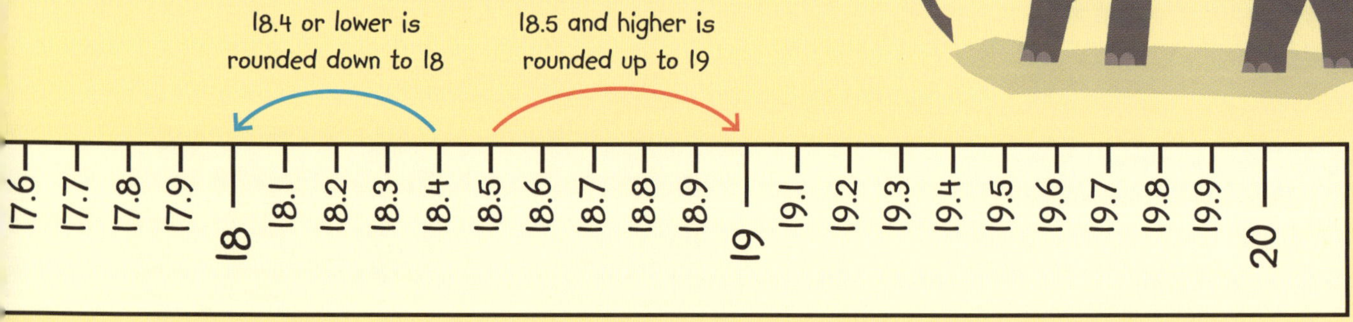

SIGNIFICANT FIGURES

When rounding, mathematicians can decide how accurate they want to be. The number of "significant figures" is how much you round the number up or down by. This could mean rounding to the nearest whole number, nearest 10, nearest 100, and so on. Imagine you wanted to round the number 1,171. Four significant figures would mean the number stays the same; three would round it down to 1,170; two would round it up to 1,200; and one would round it down to 1,000.

Significant figure	Rounded number
4	1171
3	1170
2	1200
1	1000

DECIMAL PLACES

Numbers with decimal places can also be rounded up or down. This is very handy when dealing with measurements such as distance, weight, and temperature. Usually, only two decimal places are needed.

Decimal places	Rounded number
3	8.152
2	8.15
1	8.2
0	8

ESTIMATION CALCULATIONS

Rounding is really useful if you need to do tricky operations in a hurry without a calculator. By rounding the numbers up or down, you can make the math a little easier and often still get close to the exact answer.

You might find this a tricky calculation to do in your head.

168 + 743 = 911

Rounding 168 up to 170 and 743 down to 740 might make it easier.

170 + 740 = 910

200 + 700 = 900

Adding 200 to 700 is a simple sum to do in your head. The answer, 900, is still close to the actual answer of 911.

DID YOU KNOW?

Estimating words

Have you ever wondered how many words there are in a book you're reading? You can estimate this by counting all the words on one page and then multiplying that number by the total number of pages.

TRY IT OUT

HOW TO SHOP QUICKLY

When shopping for multiple items, if you want to know their total price, you can use rounding. To simplify the numbers, round them up or down to the nearest 10 and then add them together. So the bike becomes \$160, the lights \$20, and the helmet \$50. Together, they cost roughly \$230. The actual answer is \$229.88.

When you next go shopping, try to round the numbers of the prices, add them together, and then compare your result to the actual cost.

REAL WORLD

Counting crowds

To estimate the number of people in a crowd, mathematicians use "Jacobs's method." They divide the crowd into sections and then count how many people are in one section. Then all they need to do is multiply this number by the number of sections.

HOW TO CATCH A CHEAT

In 19th-century France, mathematician Henri Poincaré visited his local baker every day for a fresh loaf of bread. The loaves were supposed to weigh 1 kg each, but Poincaré grew suspicious that the baker was cheating his customers by selling loaves that were not as heavy as everyone thought. He decided to investigate. He worked out the average, or typical, weight of a loaf and caught out the cheating baker.

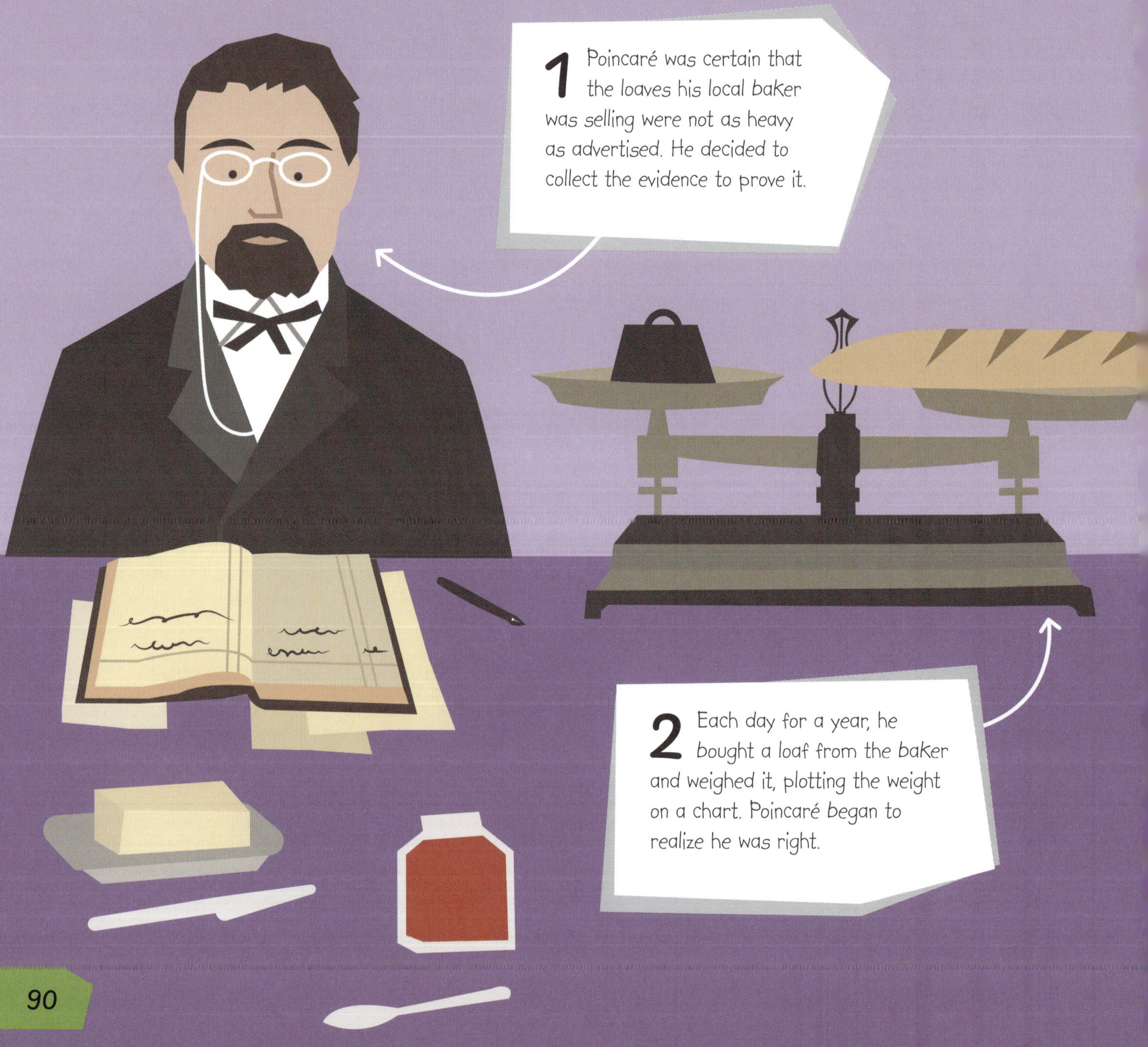

3 After a year, he worked out that the average weight of the loaves he'd bought was only 950 g—50 g less than it should have been. Poincaré went to the police, who fined the baker.

Doing the math
THE AVERAGE

To prove the baker was lying, Poincaré worked out the average weight of all the loaves of bread he'd bought. There are three types of average—the mean, the median, and the mode—but to investigate his local baker, Poincaré used the mean. To do this, he had to find the total weight of all the individual loaves. Here, just seven loaves are shown—the number he bought in a week.

$$950\,g + 955\,g + 915\,g + 960\,g + 1005\,g + 850\,g + 1015\,g = 6650\,g$$

Then, he took this combined weight and divided it by the total number of loaves.

$$\frac{6650\,g}{7} = 950\,g$$

This showed that the mean weight of the loaves he'd bought in a week was 950 g. It proved that even though some of the loaves that he'd bought weighed more than 1 kg, the mean weight was lower than advertised.

PLOTTING WEIGHTS

To provide the police with evidence, Poincaré plotted his findings on a graph that showed the various weights of bread. The graph revealed that the most common weights were grouped around 950 g.

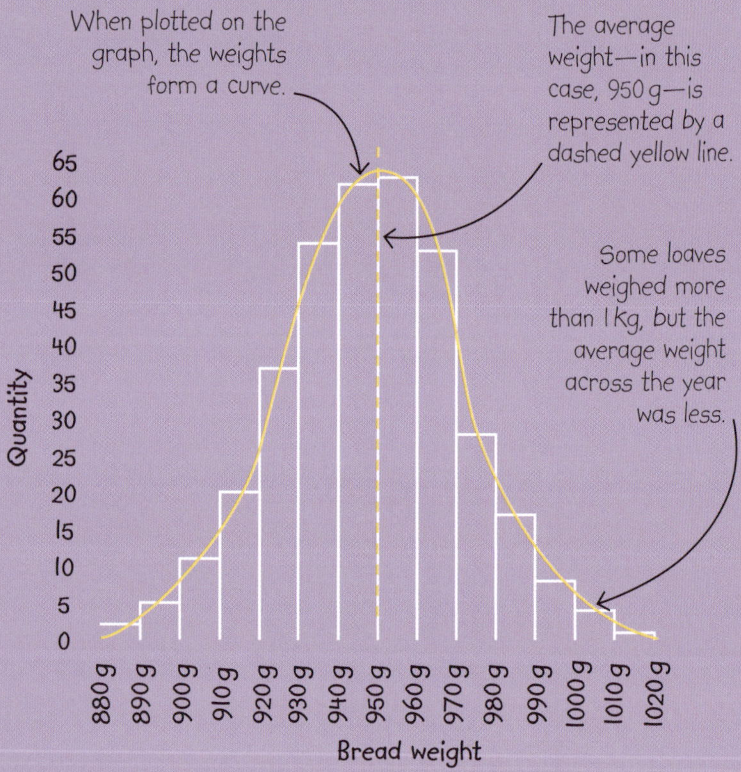

THE MEDIAN

Another way of calculating the average is by using the median. To find the median, a set of values is arranged in order—the value in the middle is the median. This is the best way of finding the average if one value in the set is much higher or lower than the rest. That's because this unusual value, or outlier, would make the mean misleading—if you wanted to know the mean weight of seven loaves but one was much heavier than the others, the mean weight would be higher than the weight of the rest of the other loaves.

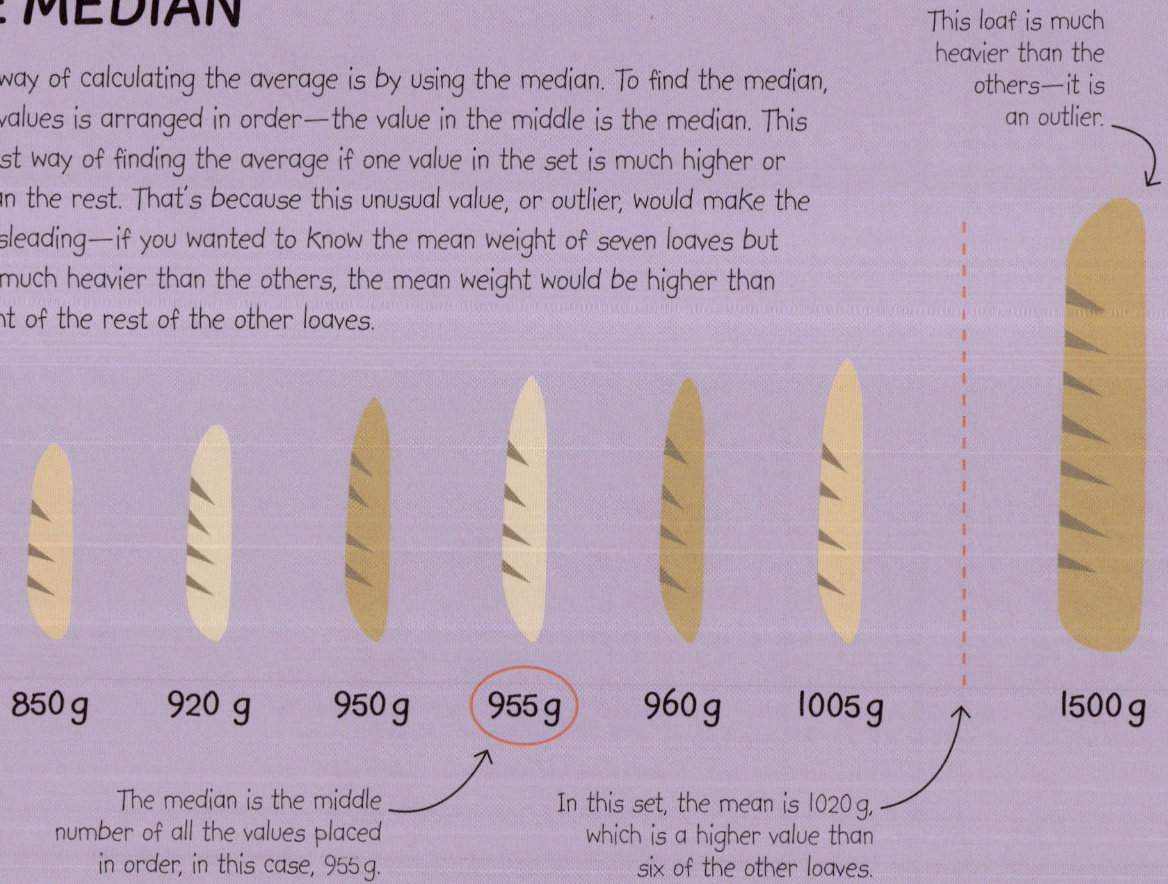

THE MODE

The mode is another type of average used by mathematicians. It is the most common value in a set of data. It is sometimes more useful than the mean or the median, for instance, if you wanted to know which cake was the most popular in the bakery.

Chocolate	7
Strawberry	6
Lemon	3

More people bought chocolate than any other cake, so it is the mode.

REAL WORLD

The wisdom of crowds

If you asked a group of people to estimate how many jelly beans are in a jar, it's likely that the median of all their answers would be pretty close to the correct number. The median is the best average to use in this example, because the mean would be distorted by some people guessing far too low and others far too high.

TRY IT OUT

HOW TO FIND THE AVERAGE HEIGHT

Imagine you want to work out the average height of children in a class. The most common way of doing it is to find the mean by adding up everybody's height and dividing the total by the number of students. For example:

$$60\text{ in} + 56\text{ in} + 63\text{ in} + 61\text{ in} + 54\text{ in} + 55\text{ in} + 61\text{ in} + 58\text{ in} + 61\text{ in} + 65\text{ in} + 55\text{ in} = 649\text{ in}$$

$$\frac{649\text{ in}}{11} = 59\text{ in}$$

Can you find the median and mode for this set of height measurements? You could then try finding out the mean, median, and mode of the heights of your own classmates.

Which type of average do you think is most useful in this case—the mean, the median, or the mode? And which is the least useful?

HOW TO ESTIMATE THE POPULATION

How do you work out the population of a country when it's impossible to count every single person? This question puzzled French mathematician Pierre-Simon Laplace, who in 1783 wondered if he could use math to accurately estimate the population of France. He came up with a brilliant solution that combined smart logic with some surprisingly simple arithmetic.

Doing the math
COLLECTING DATA SAMPLES

Laplace realized he could estimate the total population by finding out how many adults there were for each baby born. Although most towns didn't keep records of their entire population, there were some that did, and he used these to make some calculations.

The relationship between two quantities is known as a ratio. We use a colon to separate the pieces of information.

1 baby : 28 adults

2 Although most towns didn't keep track of their population, they did record how many babies were born each year.

3 Using the records from a selection of different towns, Laplace worked out that, on average, there were about 1,000,000 births per year in the whole country.

Laplace discovered that, on average, for every 28 people living in France, there was one baby born (so, among a group of 52 people, there would probably be two babies born, and so on). All he now had to do was multiply 28 by 1,000,000 (the approximate number of babies born in France that year) to reach his estimate of the total population. This method of estimating the population size became known as the "capture-recapture" method.

$$28 \times 1{,}000{,}000 = 28{,}000{,}000$$

ESTIMATING AN ANIMAL POPULATION

Laplace's method can be used to work out animal populations, too. Imagine you want to find how many birds live in an area of forest. First, gather a number of birds and tag each one. This is your first sample. Release them, and then after some time, gather a second sample. Some of the birds in the second sample will be tagged, meaning they were also in the first sample.

Sample 1: 8 birds

Each bird caught is tagged and then released to mix with the total population.

Four of the 10 birds caught in the second sample had tags on them, so they were also caught in the first sample.

Sample 2: 10 birds (4 tagged)

In the second sample, there are 10 birds in total, four of which are tagged. So the ratio of tagged birds to total birds is 4:10, which can be simplified to 1:2.5.

In the first sample, there were 8 untagged birds altogether. The relationship between tagged and untagged birds (1:2.5) in the second sample is likely to be the same for the total population in the forest. That means we need to multiply 8 by 2.5, which gives us an estimate of 20 birds.

$8 \times 2.5 = 20$ birds

REAL WORLD

Tigers in the wild

Scientists use the capture-recapture method to estimate population numbers of endangered species, such as the tiger. Scientists set up camera traps along forest trails to take photographs and, to make sure the same animals are not recounted, they identify each tiger by its unique pattern of stripes.

IMPROVING THE ESTIMATE

To get a more accurate result, you can repeat this process several times. By working out the mean of these different results, you can get a more reliable estimate.

	Number captured	Tagged	Population estimate
1st recapture	10	4	20
2nd recapture	12	6	16
3rd recapture	9	4	18

$$\text{Mean estimate} = \frac{20 + 16 + 18}{3} = 18 \text{ birds}$$

This is the number of samples taken.

Last time, we thought that there might be 20 birds. We now have a lower, more accurate estimate.

TRY IT OUT

HOW TO ESTIMATE A QUANTITY

Say you take a large lidded jar and fill it with red beads. (You don't know how many!)

You take out 40 red beads from the jar and replace them with 40 blue beads, then put the lid back on the jar and give it a good shake.

Next, you put a blindfold on and remove 50 beads from the jar. You count them out one by one and place them into a bowl.

You remove the blindfold and count how many blue beads there are in the bowl out of the total of 50 beads. There are 4.

Can you guess how many beads are in the jar in total? Use the method on the page opposite to work out the ratio and estimate the total number of beads.

HOW TO CHANGE THE WORLD WITH DATA

Between 1853 and 1856, Britain, France, Sardinia, and the Ottoman Empire fought a war against the Russian Empire. They fought in the Crimea, near the Black Sea, and tens of thousands of soldiers died. Army generals were convinced that most soldiers who died in the Crimea did so because of the injuries they received in battle. But Florence Nightingale, an English nurse, thought otherwise. She set out to prove that soldiers were actually dying because of the dirty, rat- and flea-infested conditions in the military hospitals—and she did this using data.

Doing the math

PRESENTING DATA

Instead of a table of numbers, Nightingale created a circular diagram similar to a modern-day pie chart to present her findings. Known as a coxcomb, the diagram showed that the majority of soldiers' deaths were not the result of battle wounds, but were in fact preventable if hospital conditions were improved. This simple and compelling graphic was an instant hit, and many newspapers printed it so that the public could see. By making her data easy to understand for nonmathematicians, Nightingale convinced the army generals to spend money on improving the military hospitals.

Reasons for military deaths in the Crimea (July 1854–March 1855)

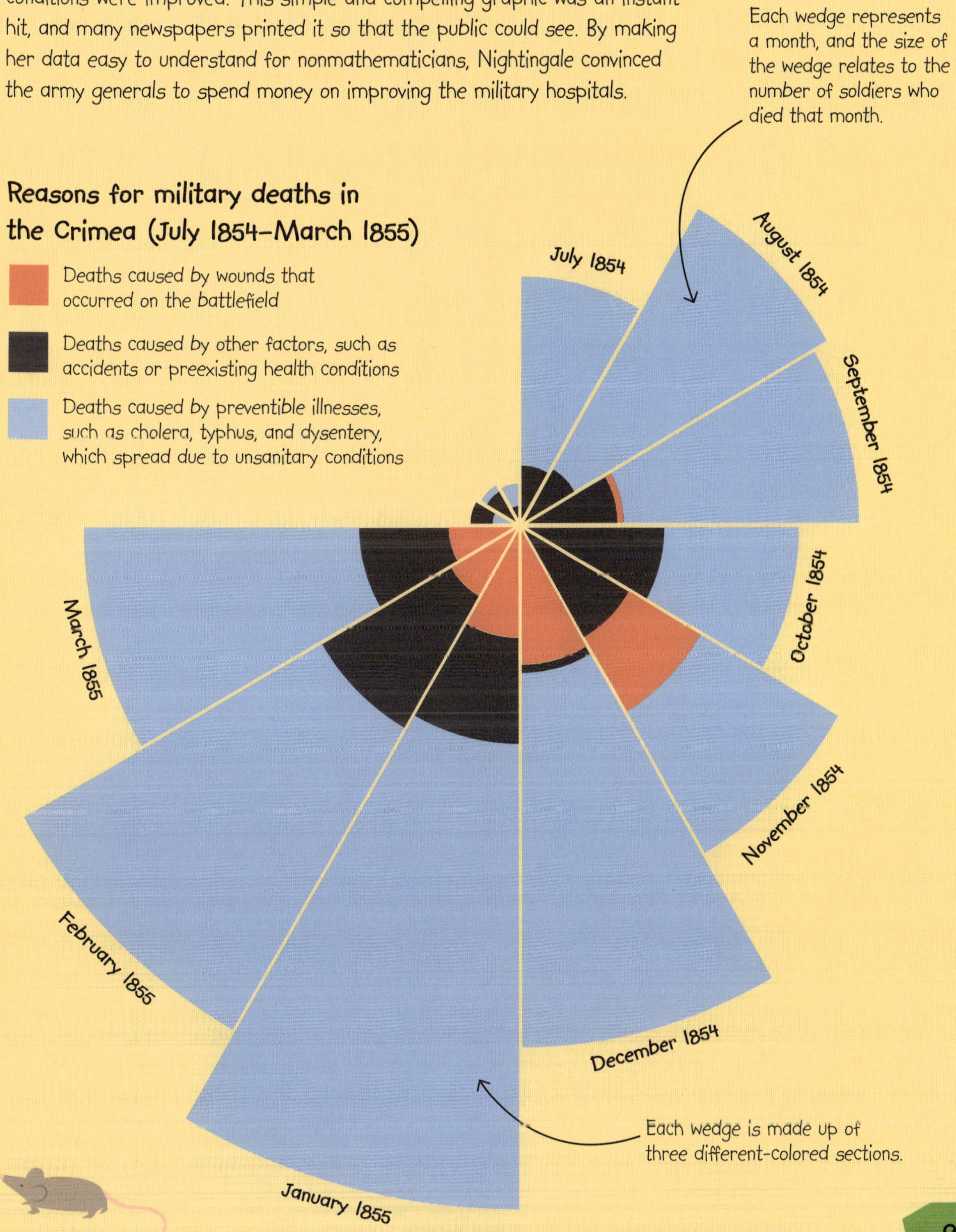

PRESENTING THE FACTS

Florence Nightingale wasn't the only one using data to campaign for reform in the 19th century. English physician John Snow and French engineer Charles Joseph Minard also made powerful arguments for changes in society by presenting data in visually exciting ways.

CURING CHOLERA

In 1854, a cholera epidemic swept through Soho in London, England, killing hundreds of people. At the time, it was thought that the disease was spread by bad smells. But physician John Snow proved that cholera was actually the result of dirty water. He did this by plotting the deaths on a map. The map showed that those who died all used the same dirty water pump. Snow's map proved that improving the cleanliness of local water supplies was the best way to prevent future outbreaks of the disease.

TRACKING LIVES LOST

In 1869, some people in France were complaining about the French army's recent lack of military victories in wars the country was fighting. Horrified, French engineer Charles Joseph Minard tried to remind them how many lives were lost because of conflict and how awful it was. His "flow map" depicts the huge numbers of French troops who died during Napoleon's campaign to attack Russia in 1812. Although fighting continued, Minard's flow map has since been highly praised for the amount of information it depicts.

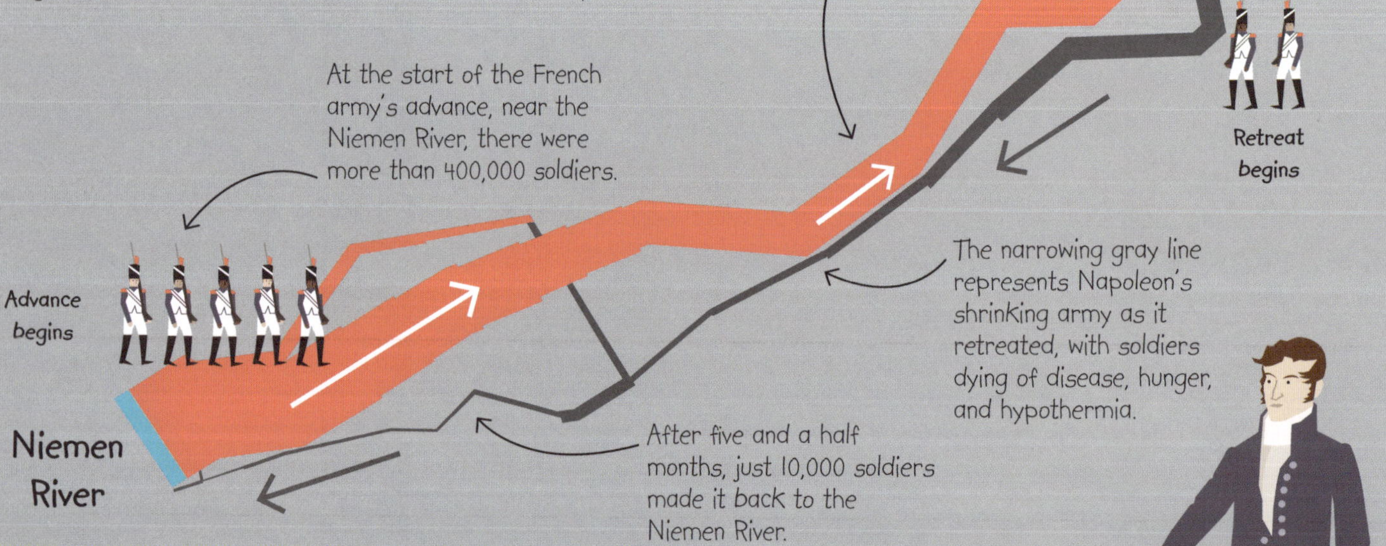

TYPES OF GRAPH

Graphs and charts present data in visual ways that are easy for us to read and understand quickly. This, in turn, makes it easier to analyze the data and find patterns or draw conclusions. For a graph to be effective, it is important to choose the best type for the information you're showing.

DID YOU KNOW?

William Playfair

In the late 1700s, Scottish engineer and secret agent William Playfair invented the bar chart and line graph. He argued that color-coded pictures explained information more clearly than tables of numbers.

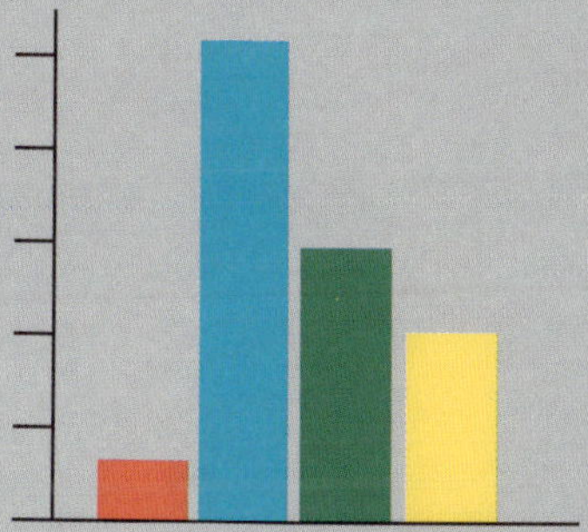

Bar chart

This common type of graph allows you to instantly compare quantities of something side by side.

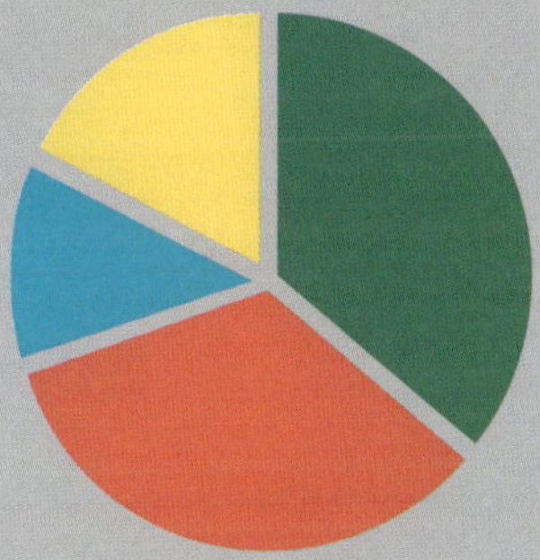

Pie chart

A pie chart is a circle divided into slices. The circle shows all the data. Each slice represents a proportion of it.

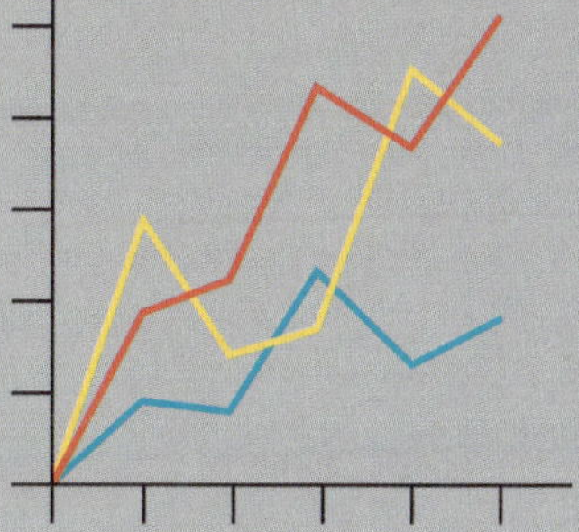

Line graph

A line graph allows you to plot data that changes over time to help you find a pattern.

TRY IT OUT

HOW TO CONVINCE YOUR PARENTS

A student is trying to convince her parents to let her go to a sleepover at the weekend. To persuade them, she must demonstrate the hard work she's put into her chores and homework, compared to leisure activities, such as watching TV and playing games. From Monday to Friday, out of a possible 20 hours, she's spent 5 hours on chores, 10 hours on homework, $2\frac{1}{2}$ hours watching TV, and $2\frac{1}{2}$ hours playing video games. She displays this data in a pie chart.

Now, make a pie chart to show your parents just how hard you've been working over the last five days.

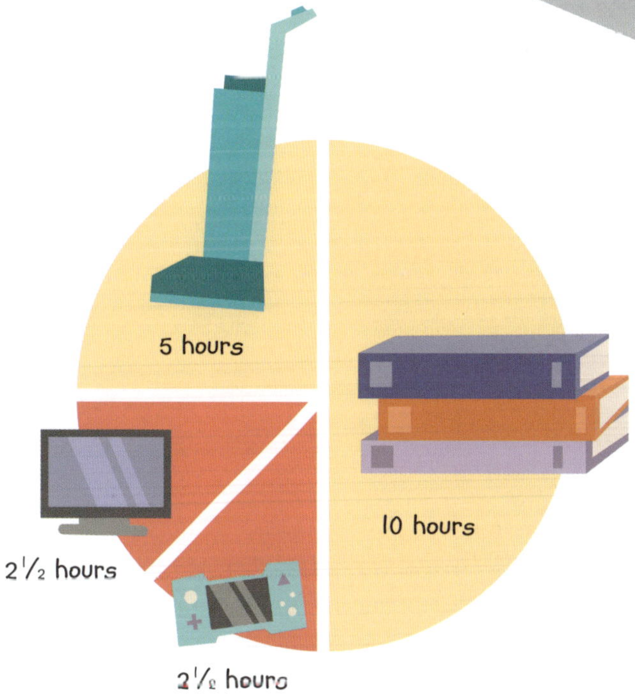

HOW TO COMPUTE BIG NUMBERS

Throughout history, people struggled to work with very big, or very small, numbers. Doing difficult calculations when you only have 10 fingers—or digits—to help was a test of brainpower. This problem led to the invention of an array of calculators, from the simple abacus to complex devices that can store instructions and operate automatically, which we now call "computers."

THE ABACUS

The earliest abacuses, used in ancient Sumeria (modern-day southern Iraq), were very different from the children's toy we think of today. They were clay slabs with five columns of increasing values written on them. Clay number tokens were placed on the appropriate columns to represent the numbers to add or subtract.

The columns were for 1s, 10s, 60s, 600s, and 3600s

7200 + 600 + 180 + 40 + 8 = 8028

c. 2700 BCE

c. 200 BCE

c. 100 BCE

Rotatable disks allowed the astrolabe's user to make calculations.

NAVIGATIONAL AID

The astrolabe was an instrument that allowed sailors and astronomers to make calculations (such as their latitude) by using the positions of the stars and sun in the sky. Islamic inventors developed it further, adding new dials and disks, allowing the astrolabe to make even more—and more accurate—computations.

GEARED CALCULATOR

A mechanical machine of brass gears was found in a 2,000-year-old shipwreck near the Greek island Antikythera in 1901. The Antikythera mechanism was able to do a host of complex calculations to predict the position of the planets and stars in the sky for any given date. It is believed to be the earliest-known computer.

When found, the mechanism was heavily damaged and fragile, having spent more than 2,000 years at the bottom of the sea.

NAPIER'S BONES

Scottish scholar John Napier created a system of rods, which were originally made of bone, to help with tricky multiplication and division. Each rod was a column of printed numbers that, along with the other rods, formed a grid system. Each rod could be moved to make calculations.

TAXING ARITHMETIC

To help his tax-collector dad with sums, French 18-year-old Blaise Pascal built the first arithmetic machine. Made from a series of gears and dials, Pascal's calculator could only do addition and wasn't always reliable, but it was the most innovative computing machine around. Pascal went on to become France's most distinguished mathematician.

1642

1837

1622

1617

BABBAGE & LOVELACE

English mathematician Charles Babbage designed an "analytical engine," which would have been steam-powered, huge, and the world's first mechanical computer if it had been fully built. Visionary mathematician Ada Lovelace wrote a sequence of mathematical instructions to program the machine. She is now recognized as the world's first computer programmer.

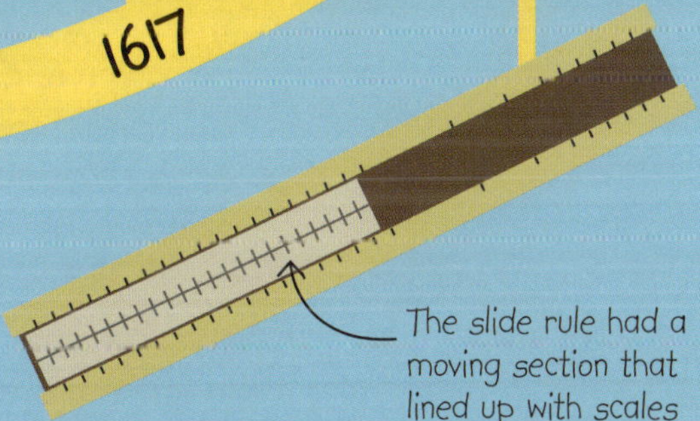

THE SLIDE RULE

English mathematician William Oughtred invented the first slide rule—a pocket-sized tool that allowed laborious calculations to be done in seconds. Its usefulness was only surpassed 350 years later by pocket electronic calculators.

TURING AND THE BOMBE

British mathematician Alan Turing aided the Allies to break German coded messages during World War II. He helped build the "Bombe," an electromechanical device that broke the codes. Many of Turing's ideas have since been incredibly influential in the development of computers.

1939–1945

POCKET POWER

Bulky, desktop-only electric calculators had been around since the late 1950s, but the microchip offered a way of shrinking them to produce portable, battery-powered calculators. The convenience of a hand-held device that did instant arithmetic made pocket calculators a smash hit.

1970

ELECTRIC COMPUTERS

Big enough to fill a room, the US Army's ENIAC was the first publicized, all-electronic, programmable computer. In 1949, EDSAC, built by a team at Cambridge University, England, became the first "real" practical computer with stored programs and could be used by nonexperts—a step toward the computers we use today.

1946

1958

MICROCHIPS

Two US electronics experts, Jack Kilby and Robert Noyce, separately thought up the microchip—an "integrated circuit" that crammed tons of electronic components onto a small silicon "chip." Microchips helped scale down the size and cost of computers but also increased their processing power. Thanks to the microchip, home computers began appearing in the 1970s.

THE INTERNET AGE

As the World Wide Web of interconnected computers was born, users needed to be able to search through the information it contained. Enter "Archie," the first internet search engine, which was developed by US student Alan Emtage. There are more than 2 billion websites online today, and lots of search engines, each with its own mathematical formula that governs how it searches.

SUPERCOMPUTERS

Extremely powerful computers are called supercomputers. The D-Wave supercomputer has the same processing power as 500 million desktop computers. Supercomputers are used to work out complex things such as weather forecasting and breaking coded messages. Another kind of powerful computing is cloud computing, where many linked computers pool their processing resources to solve problems that no one computer could do alone.

DID YOU KNOW?

Human computers

The word "computer" used to refer to humans who worked out mathematical problems with pen and paper. They were often women, and their work was of crucial importance to the success of NASA's early spaceflights.

CHESS CHAMP

Computers have gradually become more and more intelligent. A landmark moment in this trend came when computer tech giant IBM pitted their Deep Blue computer against Russian chess champion Garry Kasparov—and Deep Blue won! It was able to reason, predict moves, and numerically rate 100 million potential moves per second.

WHAT'S THE POINT OF

PROBABILITY AND LOGIC?

Using the power of logic, mathematicians can work out anything from the best route to take on a walk around town to how much of a threat a nearby asteroid might be to life on Earth. With the tools of probability, we can even predict the future by calculating how likely different outcomes might be.

HOW TO PLAN YOUR JOURNEY

In the 18th century, a particular puzzle confused the city dwellers of Königsberg (now Kaliningrad in Russia). There were seven bridges connecting the different parts of the city, but no one could work out a walking route that visited each area while crossing each bridge only once. Swiss mathematician Leonhard Euler realized the idea was impossible—the puzzle had no solution.

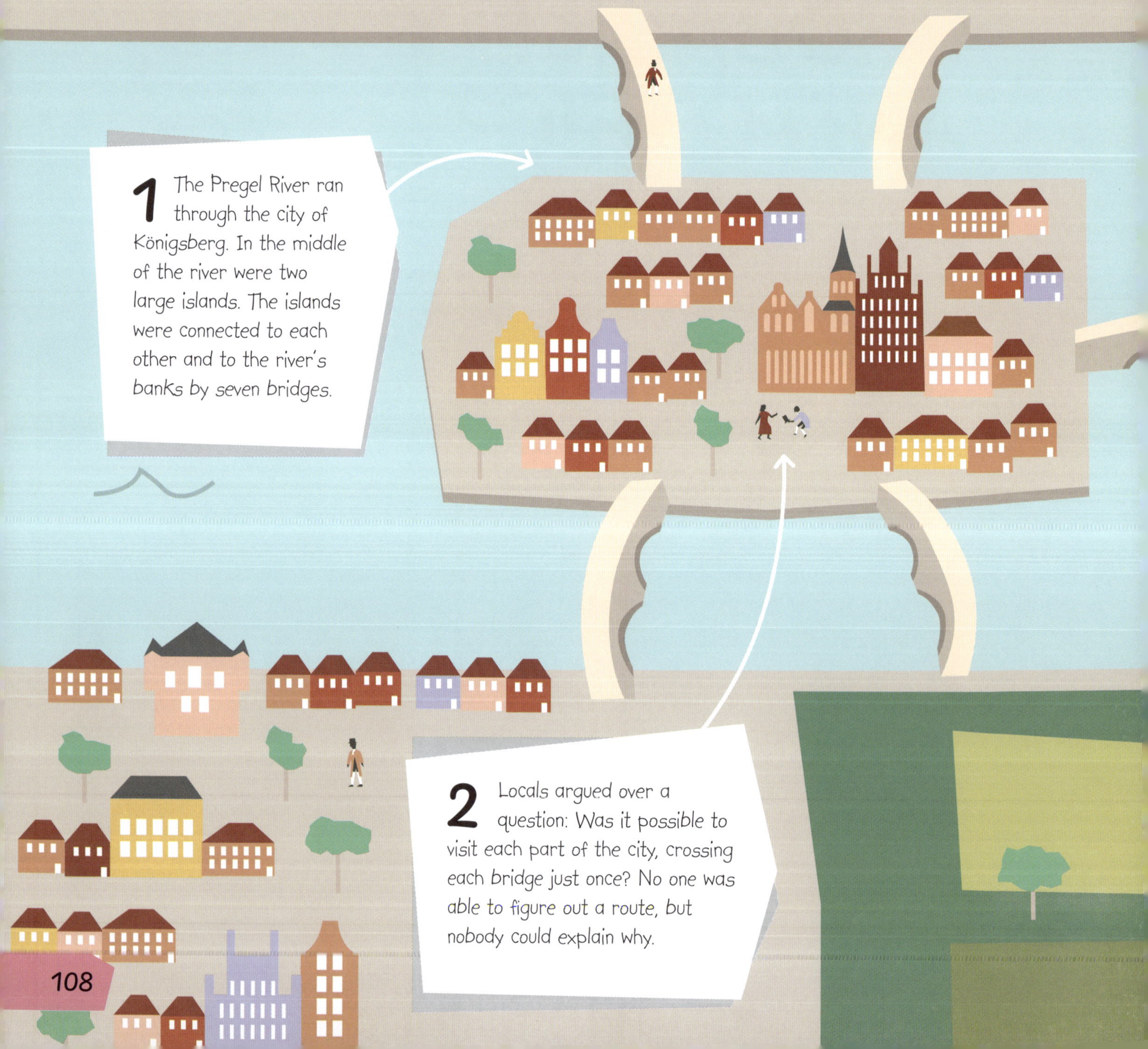

1 The Pregel River ran through the city of Königsberg. In the middle of the river were two large islands. The islands were connected to each other and to the river's banks by seven bridges.

2 Locals argued over a question: Was it possible to visit each part of the city, crossing each bridge just once? No one was able to figure out a route, but nobody could explain why.

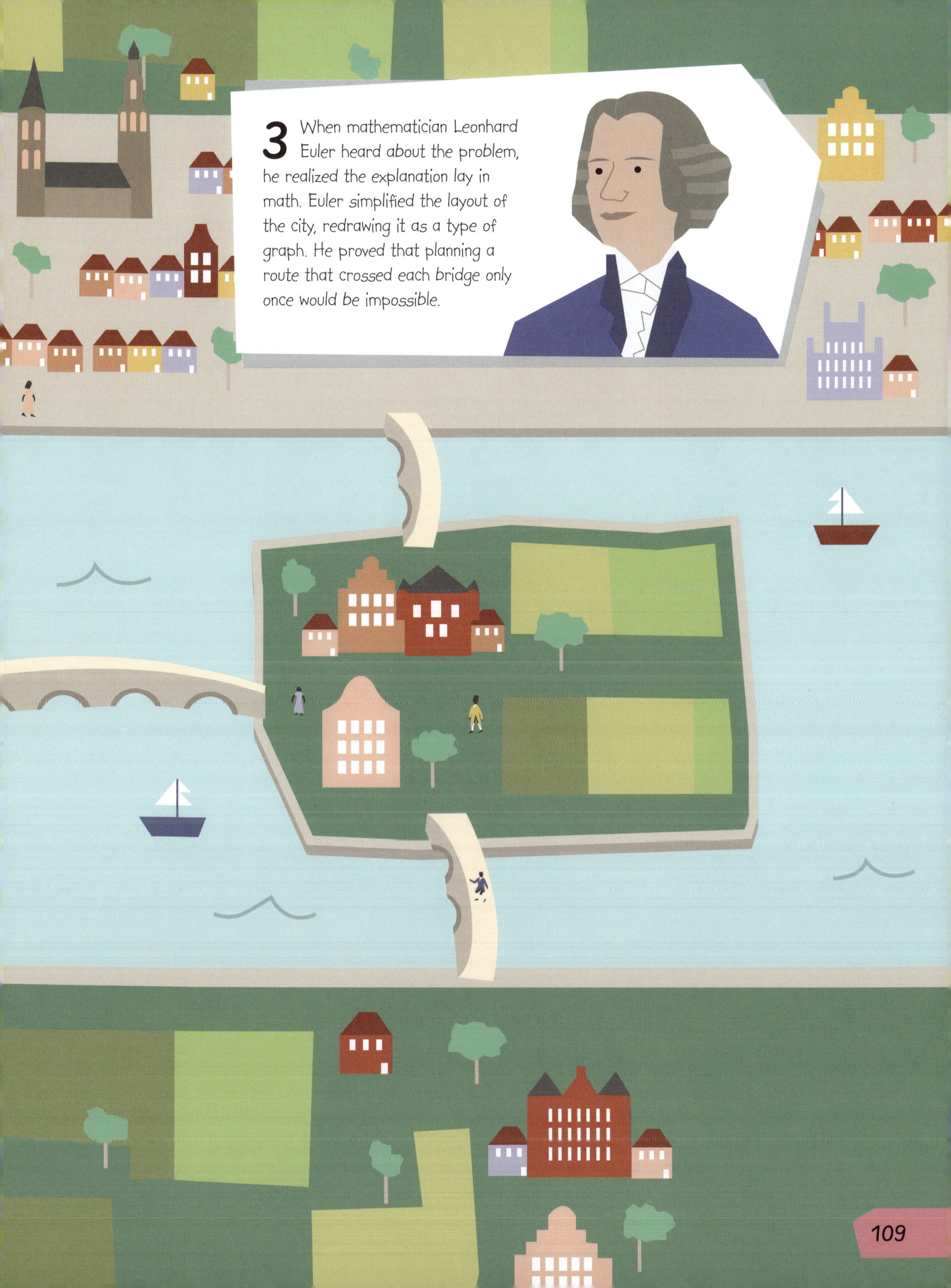

3 When mathematician Leonhard Euler heard about the problem, he realized the explanation lay in math. Euler simplified the layout of the city, redrawing it as a type of graph. He proved that planning a route that crossed each bridge only once would be impossible.

Doing the math
NETWORKS

As Euler considered the problem of the bridges, he soon realized that finding a route that worked was simply impossible. Wherever you started, you'd always end up having to cross one of the bridges twice. Euler realized that the layout of the city and the route taken didn't matter. All he needed to consider were the four areas of the city (the two islands and the two riverbanks) and the seven bridges that connected them.

Start your journey here, for example...

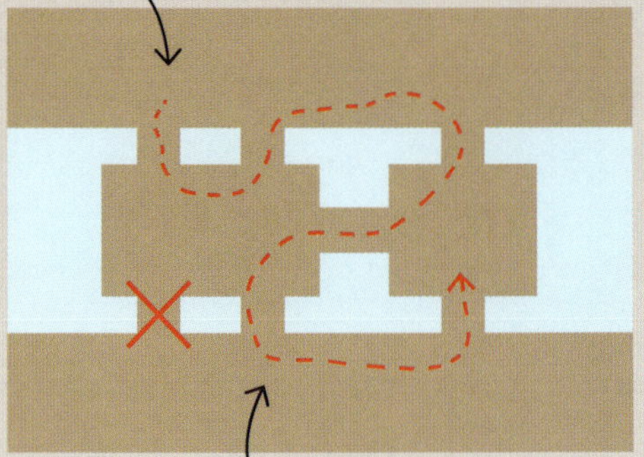

... and you'll find this path around the town won't let you cross over all the bridges.

EULERIAN PATH

Euler simplified the map and redrew it as a kind of graph, showing each area as a shape. He then added lines between them to represent the bridges. Euler noticed that all four areas of land were connected to an odd number of bridges.

IMPOSSIBLE BECAUSE...

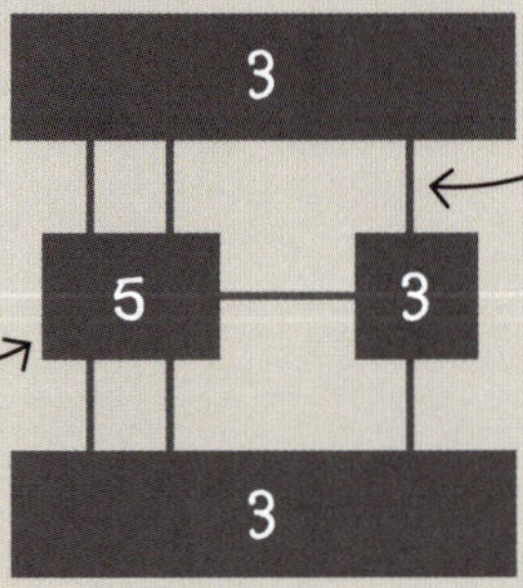

Each shape represents one of the land areas.

Each line represents a bridge.

Each area of land is marked with a number showing how many bridges connect to it.

Euler's graph shows that each area of land was connected to an odd number of bridges.

It dawned on Euler that if the puzzle had a solution—a person arriving on an area of land by a bridge had to leave by a different bridge—bridges had to exist in pairs. This meant that every area of land had to be connected by an even number of bridges, with the exception of two land areas. It was okay for two of the four areas of land to be connected by an odd number of bridges because these acted as the start and end of the route.

WOULD BE POSSIBLE IF...

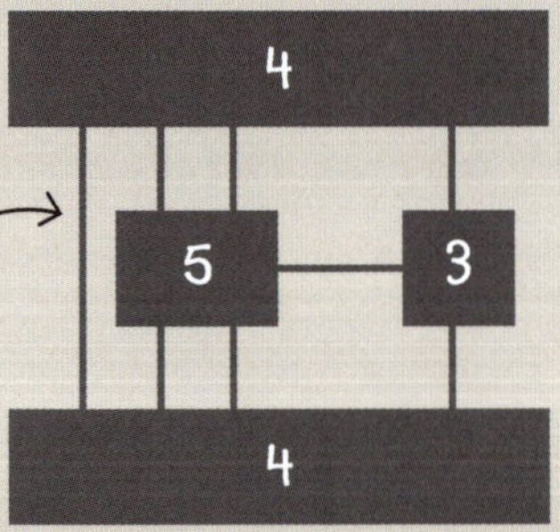

Adding a bridge would mean that only two of the land areas had an odd number of connections.

Euler proved mathematically that it was impossible to walk around the city of Königsberg crossing each bridge just once. The only solution to the problem was to make an even number of connections by adding (or subtracting) a bridge. This would make it possible to successfully walk a complete circuit and cross each bridge only once. Today, this is called an Eulerian path.

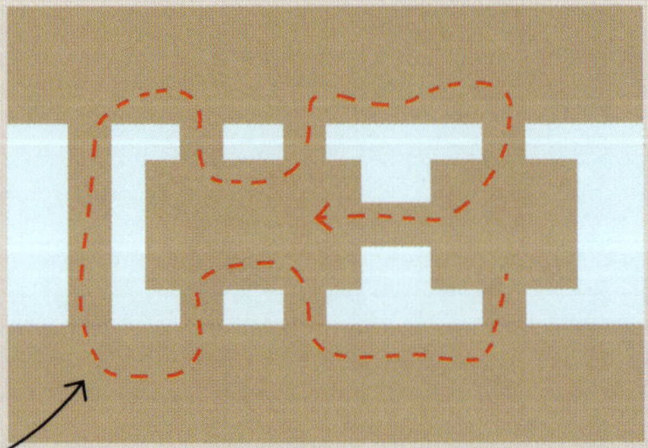

If an extra bridge was added a complete circuit would become possible.

TRY IT OUT
HOW TO FIND THE BEST ROUTE

A delivery person is trying to find the most efficient route around a town. She needs to travel down every street to make sure she visits every house. Can she travel around the town without walking down the same road twice?

The town has four roundabouts.

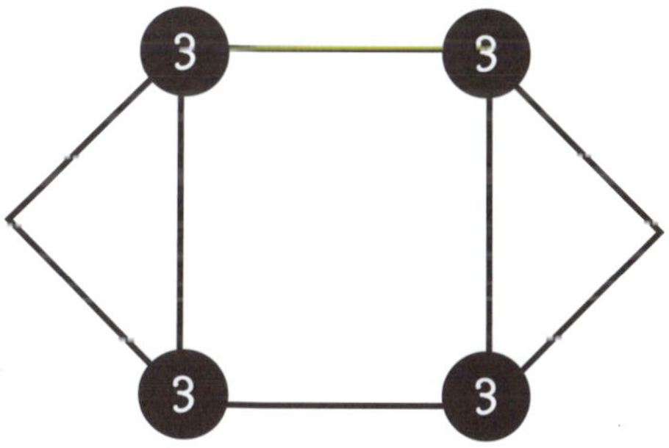

The roundabouts can be represented by black dots, each marked with the number of roads leading to it.

REAL WORLD

The World Wide Web

The World Wide Web can be thought of as a graph, like Euler's simplified map of Königsberg, with web pages equivalent to the land areas and hyperlinks equivalent to the bridges. It's a lot more complex than Euler's graph though, with billions and billions of pages and hyperlinks—and it's growing all the time!

Each roundabout has three roads coming off it. Because there are more than two roundabouts with an odd number of streets, it's impossible for the delivery person to walk around the whole town without using the same road twice.

Pick four places in your local area (perhaps your friends' houses) and try mapping a route to find the best way to make the journey between them. The route should visit each place once without going over the same part of the route twice.

PUZZLE

Which of these diagrams are successful Eulerian paths? Find out by seeing which ones you can trace, drawing over each line once and without lifting your pencil off the page.

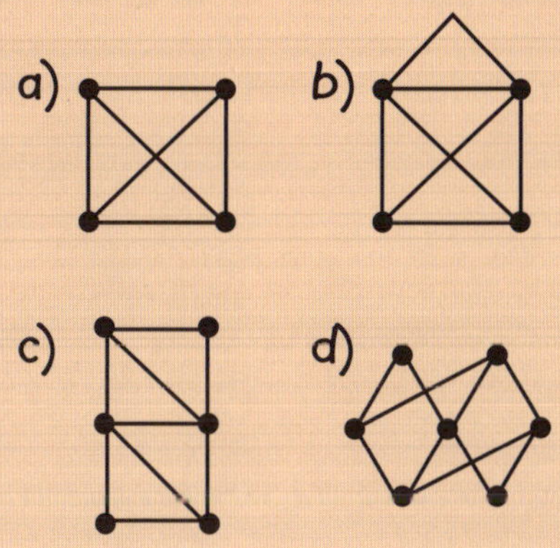

1 You're in luck! You've been selected to be a contestant on a TV game show, and there's a grand prize. The rules are simple: You'll be shown three doors, and all you need to do is pick one of them to win the prize behind it.

HOW TO WIN A GAME SHOW

Lots of TV game shows are based on luck, but is there anything you can do to improve your chance of winning? For contestants of a famous game show in the 1970s, the answer seemed illogical at first and baffled some mathematicians. The key to boosting the odds of winning lay in understanding probability, or the likelihood of something happening.

2 Behind one of the doors is the grand prize, a brand-new sports car, but behind each of the other two is a goat. Goats are nice, but let's assume you want to win the car.

3 It's time to make your choice. Dramatic music plays, the studio lights are dimmed, and a hush descends on the audience. The spotlight shines on you. You can't put the decision off any longer—the host needs an answer. You pick the blue door.

4 Before opening the blue door, the host helps you out a little by revealing one of the goats. She opens the green door—a bleating goat steps forward. The host then asks you whether you want to stick or switch—in other words, are you happy with your original choice of the blue door, or would you prefer to switch to the pink door? What do you do?

THE MONTY HALL PROBLEM

Knowing whether to stick or switch is a brain teaser called the Monty Hall problem. It is named after the host of a game show called *Let's Make a Deal*, which worked just like our game show. When the game starts, you have a $1/3$ chance of winning the car.

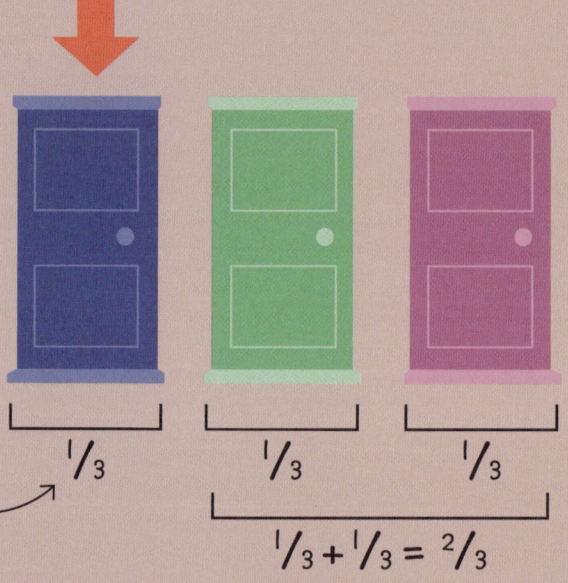

Once the host reveals that there is a goat behind the green door, you might think it doesn't matter whether you stick or switch: you now have a $1/2$ chance of winning the car. However, the original odds have not changed: there's still a $1/3$ chance the car will be behind your original pick and a $2/3$ chance it will be behind one of the other two. But now you have more information.

DID YOU KNOW?

A big deal

When you shuffle a deck of cards, it's more than likely that nobody else has ever shuffled a deck into the exact same order ever before. There are 80,658,175,170,943,878,571, 660,636,856,403,766,975,289,505,440,883,277, 824,000,000,000,000 possible combinations, so the probability of a deck being shuffled in the same way twice is astonishingly small.

STICK OR SWITCH?

Now you know that the chance of the car being behind the green door is zero. Therefore, the $^2/_3$ chance of the car being behind the two doors you didn't pick becomes "concentrated" on the pink door. To maximize your chance of winning the car, you should therefore switch. You won't win every time you play, but by switching doors, you can expect to win twice as often as you lose.

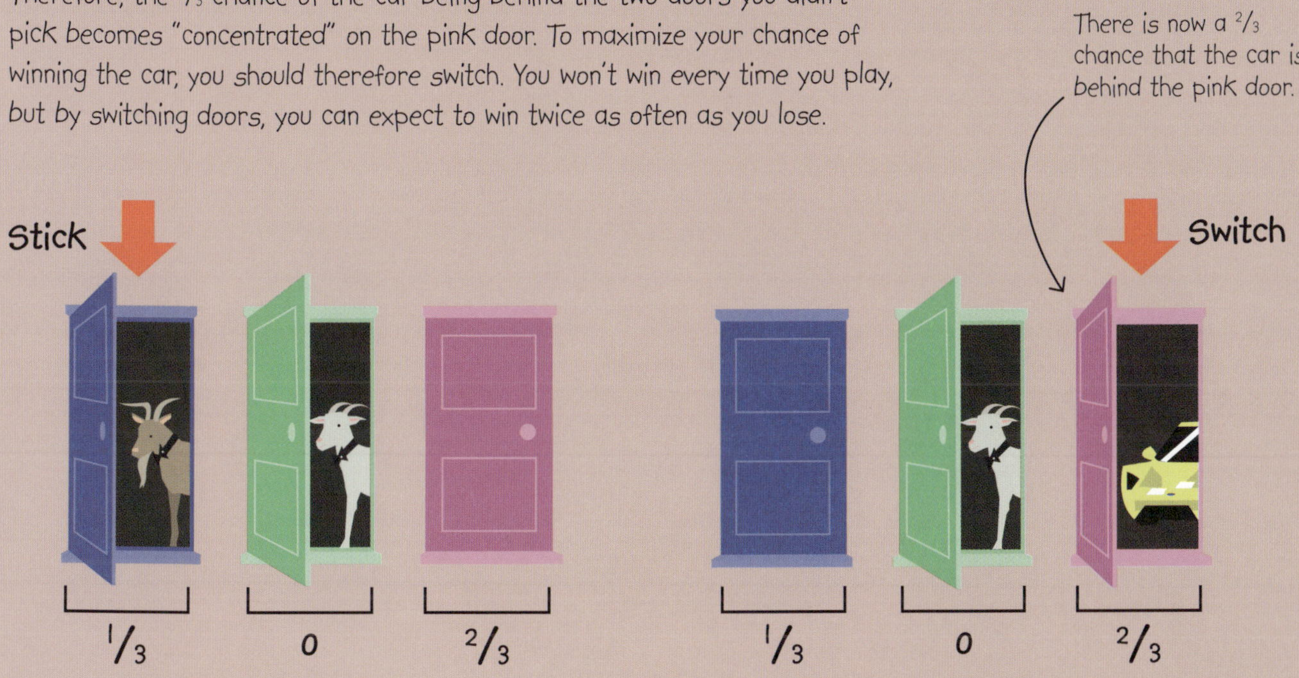

TRY IT OUT

HOW TO WORK OUT THE ODDS

Your friend flips two fair coins. (A fair coin is one where heads and tails are equally likely outcomes.) They don't tell you the outcome, but at least one of the coins lands heads.

What is the probability that the other coin also lands heads?

The answer is not $^1/_2$! To see this, write out the four possibilities for the two flips:

H-H (heads-heads)

H-T (heads-tails)

T-H (tails-heads)

T-T (tails-tails)

From the information, we can cross out T-T because one of the flips has already landed heads. This leaves three possibilities: H-H, H-T, T-H. In one out of those three cases, the other coin also lands heads and in the other two cases it lands tails. So the probability that the other coin is also a heads is actually only $^1/_3$.

Now try rolling two fair six-sided dice. One of them is a 6. What is the probability that the other one is also a 6?

REAL WORLD

Asteroid hit

Whenever an asteroid gets too close to Earth for comfort, scientists estimate the probability that it will collide with the planet. Fortunately, the probability is usually very low!

HOW TO ESCAPE PRISON

The police have arrested two men and charged them with robbing a bank. There's not enough evidence to convict either man of stealing money, but there is proof that they both broke into the bank. As the prisoners wait in their cells to be interviewed by the police, each has to decide what to say. Each can blame the other for stealing the money in the hope of walking free, or keep quiet in return for a shorter sentence for trespassing. Should each prisoner blame his accomplice or keep quiet?

3 If each prisoner blames the other for stealing the money, they each serve a sentence of 10 years in prison.

4 If Prisoner B stays silent but Prisoner A blames him for stealing the money, then Prisoner B will serve a 10-year sentence while Prisoner A will walk free for helping the police. The opposite will happen if Prisoner A remains silent while Prisoner B talks.

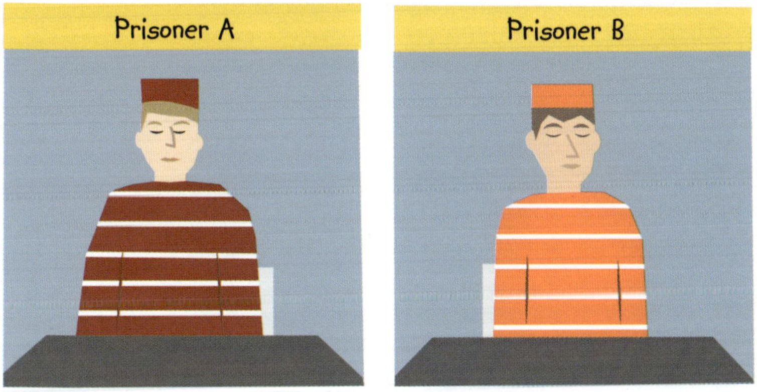

5 If they both stay silent about stealing the money, they will each be charged with breaking in and receive a shorter sentence of 2 years.

A PAYOFF MATRIX

Imagine you're Prisoner A. You don't know what Prisoner B is going to do, but what should you do to try to secure the shortest sentence for yourself? A payoff matrix weighs up all the possible strategies on offer and helps you decide how to make the best of your situation.

If you both blame each other, you'll both be convicted for stealing. You will each face a 10-year sentence—the worst possible outcome.

If you stay silent but Prisoner B blames you, he could go free while you end up serving 10 years!

		Prisoner A	
		Blames	Stays silent
Prisoner B	Blames	Both prisoners get 10 years for stealing.	Prisoner A gets 10 years for stealing money. Prisoner B goes free.
	Stays silent	Prisoner A goes free. Prisoner B gets 10 years for stealing money.	Both prisoners get 2 years for breaking in.

If both of you stay silent, neither of you can be convicted for stealing. This will achieve the best outcome for both of you—a shorter sentence.

By blaming the other prisoner, there's a chance you might walk free while Prisoner B gets 10 years. But it's a gamble: if he blames you, too, you'll both get the full sentence.

GAME THEORY

This brain teaser is called the prisoner's dilemma. It is an example of game theory, in which mathematicians imagine life as a game with winners and losers. In game theory, each individual uses strategies to try to secure the best outcome for themselves. Governments, businesses, and other organizations use game theory to try to predict how people make decisions in real life. For example, a company may use game theory when deciding how to price a product.

TRY IT OUT

RIVAL LEMONADE STALLS

Outside the school grounds one day, two stallholders open rival lemonade stalls. Each decides to charge $1 for a glass of lemonade. There are 40 customers in total, shared equally between the two stalls—20 customers prefer stall A and 20 prefer stall B.

If one stallholder cuts the price to 75¢, they will take all their competitor's customers but will make less money from each glass of lemonade. If both stallholders cut their prices, each will continue to share 50 percent of the customers, but both will still sell the same amount of lemonade and will therefore make less money.

Can you design a payoff matrix to work out how each stallholder can maximize the amount of money they can make?

Lemonade stall A

Lemonade stall B

REAL WORLD

Vampire bats

Female vampire bats work together for the common good. Although it means they will have less for themselves, vampire bats that have had their nightly meal of blood give some away to other bats that have been unable to find prey. They make this donation because when they miss a nightly meal, they'll receive blood in turn themselves. A vampire bat will die if it misses two nightly meals in a row, so this spirit of cooperation ensures the species' survival.

HOW TO MAKE HISTORY

From using a calculator and knowing the time to finding our way and using the internet, math and mathematical inventions are essential parts of our everyday lives. For that, we have a huge number of mathematicians throughout history to thank. The people in this timeline are just some of the mathematicians who have advanced human knowledge with math ideas that help in all sorts of fields—from construction and physics to navigation and space exploration.

HYPATIA

c.350–415 CE

Scholars traveled far and wide to learn from Hypatia of Alexandria, Egypt. She reworked ancient mathematical texts to make them easier to understand.

LIU HUI

3rd century CE

One of ancient China's most famous mathematicians, Liu Hui published rules for working with negative numbers. His studies helped advance the fields of construction and mapmaking.

MUHAMMAD AL-KHWARIZMI

780–850

Known as the "father of algebra," Al-Khwarizmi lived and worked in the city of Baghdad (in modern-day Iraq). He wrote *Al-jabr w'al-muqabala*, one of the earliest books on algebra. He also helped establish the widespread use of Hindu-Arabic numerals.

FIBONACCI

1170–1240

Italian mathematician Fibonacci introduced the number 0 to Europe from North Africa, but he is best known for his description of a particular sequence, now known as the "Fibonacci sequence," in which each number is the sum of the two numbers that came before it.

PYTHAGORAS

Described as the first mathematician, Pythagoras, who lived in ancient Greece, believed everything could be explained with math. A keen lyre player, he used mathematics to explain how the harplike stringed instrument worked.

c.570–495 BCE

EUCLID

Euclid, an ancient Greek mathematician, defined the rules of math relating to shapes, a field of study which became known as geometry. Euclid is called the "father of geometry."

4th century BCE

ARCHIMEDES

Ancient Greek inventor Archimedes used mathematical principles to design innovative machines, such as a giant catapult. He also discovered the principle of displacement, after realizing that the amount of water that overflowed from his bathtub was proportional to how much of his body was submerged.

c.288–212 BCE

MADHAVA OF SANGAMAGRAMA

Despite most of his work being lost to history, we do know that Indian-born Madhava was a pioneering mathematician, because others referenced his work. He founded the Kerala School of Astronomy and Mathematics in India.

c.1340–1425

LEONARDO DA VINCI

This Italian painter was also a mathematician. With great precision, da Vinci used calculations and the rules of geometry to work out perspective and proportion in his paintings rather than simply drawing by eye.

1452–1519

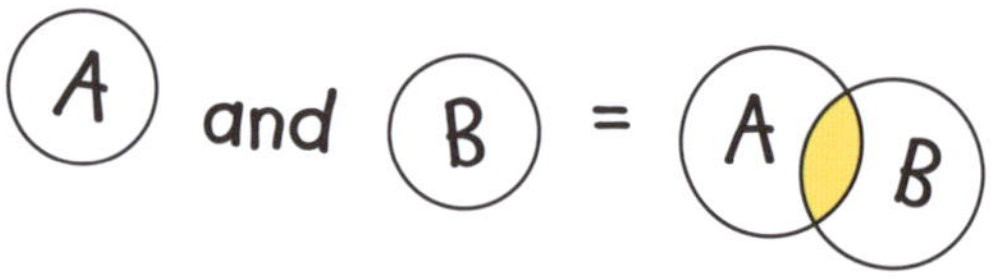

GEORGE BOOLE

English mathematician George Boole applied math to the philosophical idea of "logic" with the goal of writing complex thoughts as simple equations—the first step toward artificial intelligence.

1815–1864

JAMES CLERK MAXWELL

From Scotland, James Clerk Maxwell used mathematical methods to investigate and explain the answers to scientific questions. He discovered the existence of electromagnetic waves, later making possible the invention of radio, television, and cellphones.

1831–1879

ADA LOVELACE

Born in England, the world's first computer programmer, Augusta Ada Lovelace, translated a paper on Charles Babbage's "analytical machine." Adding her own insightful notes, she described the far-reaching possibilities of the machine.

1815–1852

SOPHIE GERMAIN

As a woman, French-born Sophie Germain was prevented from attending college, but she used a fake name to communicate with other mathematicians. She worked out a partial proof to a puzzle known as "Fermat's last theorem." The puzzle's name comes from Frenchman Pierre de Fermat, who claimed to have solved it before he died in 1665, but left no explanation of how he did it.

1776–1831

PIERRE DE FERMAT

French lawyer Pierre de Fermat studied math in his spare time. He came up with the theory of probability with Blaise Pascal and developed a way to find the highest and lowest points of curves, which Isaac Newton later used to invent calculus (the study of continuous change).

1601–1665

BLAISE PASCAL

As well as working on probability theory with Pierre de Fermat, Frenchman Pascal created the field of projective geometry (the study of lines and points). He also invented the first calculator to help his dad, who was a tax official.

1623–1662

G. H. HARDY

English mathematician Godfrey Harold Hardy was a supporter of studying math for pleasure instead of seeking to apply math in other fields, such as science, engineering, and business, although his work has helped scientists make discoveries about genes.

1877–1947

EMMY NOETHER

German-born Emmy Noether's work became the basis of modern physics; using mathematics, she made revisions to the work of German-born physicist Albert Einstein, helping to solve problems in his theories. Her work led to the creation of a new topic in math: abstract algebra.

1882–1935

MARIA GAETANA AGNESI

Italian-born Maria Agnesi was the first woman appointed as a mathematics professor at a university—the University of Bologna. She also wrote a popular math textbook.

1718–1799

ÉMILIE DU CHÂTELET

Émilie du Châtelet used her family's high social status in France to study mathematics, spending some of her money on textbooks. She translated Isaac Newton's writings into French, adding her own useful notes, in addition to writing her own mathematical book.

1706–1749

ISAAC NEWTON

English mathematician Isaac Newton created a new type of math, known as calculus, which made it possible to tackle more difficult math problems. Using mathematical methods, he investigated the movements of the planets and the speed of sound. He famously explained gravity using math.

1642–1727

GOTTFRIED LEIBNIZ

Gottfried Leibniz from Germany was the first to publish calculus theory. Although the attribution of the invention of calculus lies with Isaac Newton, mathematicians today use Leibniz's notation (way of representing the math). He developed the binary number system (sequences of 1s and 0s). This system would later form the basis of all modern computers.

1646–1716

SRINIVASA RAMANUJAN

This self-taught Indian prodigy wrote letters full of remarkable theories to other mathematicians. Recognizing Ramanujan's brilliance, English professor G. H. Hardy invited him to Cambridge University, England, to work with him. Under Hardy's guidance, Ramanujan proved thousands of tricky theories. His work also helped advance the speed of computer algorithms (step-by-step processes).

1887–1920

JOHN VON NEUMANN

Hungarian-born John von Neumann invented "game theory," a way of using math to find the best strategy in a game or tricky situation. In the US, he was key to advancing the development of the atomic bomb. He also championed the use of computers in math, and his work helped to improve their programming.

1903–1957

KATHERINE JOHNSON

In the US, Katherine Johnson worked for NASA, carrying out the calculations needed to put an astronaut on the Moon. She co-published work about safely returning the astronauts to Earth afterward.

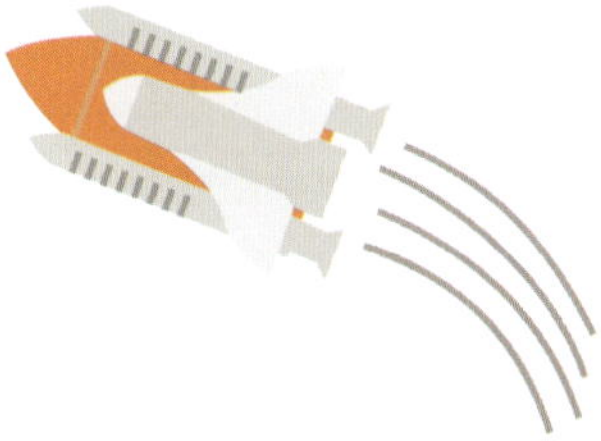

1918–2020

BENOIT MANDELBROT

Coining the term "fractals" from the Latin word for "broken," Polish-born Benoit Mandelbrot applied it to explain nonsymmetry in nature (such as that of clouds and coastlines) in mathematical terms. The math formulas behind his fractal geometry showed order in the disorderly.

1924–2010

ANDREW JOHN WILES

Fascinated by Fermat's last theorem from a young age, English mathematician Andrew John Wiles finally untangled and solved the 358-year-old math problem after 7 years of working on it and nothing else.

1953–

GRACE HOPPER

Grace Hopper worked as a college lecturer before joining the US Navy and rising to the rank of Rear Admiral. She advanced the field of computer science by devising the user-friendly programming language "COBOL," making computers more accessible to nonmathematicians.

1906–1992

ALAN TURING

English mathematician Alan Turing proposed a theoretical "computer," the Turing machine, to show that all math could be worked out if it was turned into an algorithm. During World War II, he worked to decipher encrypted German military secrets.

1912–1954

EDWARD LORENZ

US mathematician Edward Lorenz posed the question, "Does the flap of a butterfly's wings in Brazil set off a tornado in Texas?" He observed that unordered or chaotic events start out predictable, but the further you get from the starting point, the more random they appear to be.

1917–2008

PAUL ERDŐS

Eccentric Hungarian mathematician Erdős packed his life into a suitcase and traveled the world for 50 years, staying and working with other mathematicians along the way. In his lifetime, he published mathematical papers on many different topics. He had a particular passion for prime numbers.

1913–1996

MARYAM MIRZAKHANI

Informed by a teacher that she was no good at math, Iranian-born Maryam Mirzakhani proved that teacher very wrong. In 2014, her work led to her becoming the first woman to win the highly esteemed Fields Medal for her contribution to the world of mathematics. Her studies tackled the math of curved surfaces.

1977–2017

EMMA HARUKA IWAO

In 2019, on International Pi Day, Japanese Google employee Emma Haruka Iwao calculated the value of pi to a world-record accuracy of 31 trillion digits. To achieve the calculation, Iwao used a total of 170 terabytes of data from 25 computers linked virtually by Google's cloud system over a course of 121 days.

1986–

GLOSSARY

ALGEBRA
The use of letters or other symbols to stand for unknown quantities when making calculations.

ANGLE
The amount of turn from one direction to another. You can also think of it as the difference in direction between two lines meeting at a point. Angles are measured in degrees.

ARITHMETIC SEQUENCE
A pattern in which the numbers increase (or decrease) by a fixed amount each time.

AVERAGE
The typical or middle value of a set of data. There are different kind of averages. See mean, median, and mode.

AXIS
One of the lines of a grid used to measure the position of points and shapes. An axis of symmetry is another name for a line of symmetry.

BINARY SYSTEM
A number system with only two digits: 0 and 1. Digital devices store and process data in binary form.

CIPHER
Where individual letters in a piece of text are substituted with another letter, number, or symbol to hide the meaning of the text.

CODE
A system of letters, numbers, or symbols used to replace whole words to hide their meaning.

COMMON DIFFERENCE
The fixed amount by which an arithmetic sequence increases or decreases.

COMMON RATIO
The fixed amount by which the numbers in a geometric sequence are multiplied to give the next number in the sequence.

COMPUTER
An electronic device for making calculations and storing data; also, in the past, a person who made calculations.

COMPUTING
Using computers to carry out calculations.

COORDINATES
Pairs of numbers that describe the position of a point, line, or shape on a grid or the position of something on a map.

CRYPTOGRAPHY
The study of making and breaking codes.

DATA
Any information that has been collected to be analyzed.

DECIMAL
Relating to the number 10 (and to tenths, hundredths, and so on). A decimal fraction (also called a decimal) is written using a dot called a decimal point. The numbers to the right of the dot are tenths, hundredths, and so on. For example, a quarter ($^1/_4$) as a decimal is 0.25, which means 0 ones, 2 tenths, and 5 hundredths.

DIGIT
The written symbols 0–9 that are used to write out a number.

EQUATION
A statement in math that something equals something else—for example, $2 + 2 = 4$.

ESTIMATE
To find an answer that's close to the correct answer, often by rounding one or more numbers up or down.

FORMULA
A rule or statement written with mathematical symbols.

FRACTION
A part of a whole quantity or number.

GEOMETRIC SEQUENCE
A sequence that increases by multiplying each number by a common ratio.

GEOMETRY
The area of math that explores shapes, size, and space.

GRAPH
A diagram that shows the relationship between two or more sets of numbers or measurements.

INFINITY
A number that is larger than any other number and can never be given an exact value.

LATITUDE
A measure of how far north or south of the equator you are. The latitude of the equator is 0°, while the North Pole has a latitude of +90° and the South Pole has a latitude of −90°.

MEAN
An average found by adding up the values in a set of data and dividing by the number of values.

MEDIAN
The middle value of a set of data, when the values are ordered from lowest to highest.

MODE
The number that appears most often in a set of data.

PARALLEL
Two straight lines are parallel if they are always the same distance apart.

PERCENTAGE
The number of parts out of 100. Percentage is shown by the symbol %.

PI
The circumference of any circle divided by its diameter always gives the same value, which we call pi. It is represented by the Greek symbol π.

POWER
A small number written at the top right of a base number. It indicates how many times you should multiply the base number by itself.

PRIME NUMBER
A number that has exactly two factors: 1 and itself. The first 10 prime numbers are 2, 3, 5, 7, 11, 13, 17, 19, 23, and 29.

PROBABILITY
The likelihood that something will happen.

PROCESSING POWER
The speed at which a computer can perform an operation. The more processing power a computer has, the more calculations it can carry out in a set period of time.

PROOF
A mathematical argument that demonstrates that a theory is true.

PROPORTION
A part or share of something considered in relation to its whole.

RATIO
The relationship between two numbers, expressed as the number of times one is bigger or smaller than another.

RIGHT ANGLE
An angle that is exactly 90 degrees.

SAMPLE
A part of a whole group from which data is collected to give information about the group.

SEQUENCE
A list of numbers generated according to a rule—for example, 2, 4, 6, 8, 10.

SYMMETRY
A shape or object has symmetry (or is described as symmetrical) if it looks unchanged after it has been partially rotated, reflected, or translated (moved).

THREE-DIMENSIONAL
The term used to describe objects that have height, width, and depth.

TWO-DIMENSIONAL
The term used to describe flat objects that have only width and length.

WHOLE NUMBER
The numbers 1, 2, 3, 4, 5, and so on, as well as zero.

ANSWERS

Page 13
38, 25, 16

Page 27
262°F and 146°C

Page 30
$32

Page 35
9

Page 63
The treasure is buried at (6,4).

Page 67
The next number in the sequence is 142.

Page 69
We know that $a = 12$, $d = 2$, and $n = 15$.
$12 + (15 - 1) \times 2 =$ 40 seats

Page 72
Nine quintillion, two hundred and twenty-three quadrillion, three hundred and seventy-two trillion, thirty-six billion, eight hundred and fifty-four million, seven hundred and seventy-five thousand, eight hundred and eight.

Page 73
$1 \times 2^{(20-1)} = 1 \times 2^{19} = 524{,}288$

$2 \times 3^{(15-1)} = 2 \times 3^{14}$
$= 9{,}565{,}938$ coins

Page 75
$31 \times 19 = 589$

Page 79
Shifting the letters backward three spaces recovers the original message: WE ARE NOT ALONE.

Page 93
The median height is 60 in. The mode height is 61 in. The mean is the most useful average. The mode is the least useful.

Page 97
Four blue beads out of a total of 50 beads in the second sample gives you a ratio of 4:50, which can be simplified to 1:12.5. Multiply 40 (the total number of beads in the first sample) by 12.5 to make an estimate of 500 beads in total.

Page 111
Graphs b and c are possible. Start and end at the dots with an odd number of connections.

Page 115
There are 11 possible combinations if one die rolls a 6: 1-6, 2-6, 3-6, 4-6, 5-6, 6-6, 6-5, 6-4, 6-3, 6-2, and 6-1. Therefore, the probability is 1 in 11.

Page 119

		Stall A	
		Keeps price at $1	Drops price to 75¢
Stall B	Keeps price at $1	Both stallholders sell 20 glasses of lemonade and make $20 each, or $40 in total. This is the best overall outcome.	Stallholder A gets all the customers and sells 40 glasses of lemonade for $30. Stallholder B makes nothing.
	Drops price to 75¢	Stallholder B gets all the customers and sells 40 glasses of lemonade for $30. Stallholder A makes nothing.	Both stallholders sell 20 glasses of lemonade and make $15 each, or $30 in total.